T0380559

Cambridge Elements ≡

Elements in European Politics
edited by
Catherine De Vries
Bocconi University
Gary Marks
University of North Carolina at Chapel Hill and European University Institute

DEMAND FOR EU POLITY BUILDING IN THE SHADOW OF THE RUSSIAN THREAT

Ioana-Elena Oana
European University Institute

Alexandru D. Moise
European University Institute

Zbigniew Truchlewski
University of Amsterdam
European University Institute
London School of Economics and Political Science

Shaftesbury Road, Cambridge CB2 8EA, United Kingdom

One Liberty Plaza, 20th Floor, New York, NY 10006, USA

477 Williamstown Road, Port Melbourne, VIC 3207, Australia

314–321, 3rd Floor, Plot 3, Splendor Forum, Jasola District Centre,
New Delhi – 110025, India

103 Penang Road, #05–06/07, Visioncrest Commercial, Singapore 238467

Cambridge University Press is part of Cambridge University Press & Assessment,
a department of the University of Cambridge.

We share the University's mission to contribute to society through the pursuit of
education, learning and research at the highest international levels of excellence.

www.cambridge.org
Information on this title: www.cambridge.org/9781009497602

DOI: 10.1017/9781009497596

First published 2025

A catalogue record for this publication is available from the British Library

ISBN 978-1-009-49760-2 Hardback
ISBN 978-1-009-49762-6 Paperback
ISSN 2754-5032 (online)
ISSN 2754-5024 (print)

Additional resources for this publication at www.cambridge.org/polity_building

Cambridge University Press & Assessment has no responsibility for the persistence
or accuracy of URLs for external or third-party internet websites referred to in this
publication and does not guarantee that any content on such websites is, or will
remain, accurate or appropriate.

Demand for EU Polity Building in the Shadow of the Russian Threat

Elements in European Politics

DOI: 10.1017/9781009497596
First published online: March 2025

Ioana-Elena Oana
European University Institute

Alexandru D. Moise
European University Institute

Zbigniew Truchlewski
University of Amsterdam
European University Institute
London School of Economics and Political Science

Author for correspondence: Ioana-Elena Oana, ioana.oana@eui.eu

Abstract: The Russian invasion of Ukraine came on the heels of a series of crises that tested the resilience of the EU as a compound polity and arguably re-shaped European policymaking at all levels. This Element investigates the effects of the invasion on public support for European polity building across four key policy domains: refugee policy, energy policy, foreign policy, and defence. It shows how support varies across four polity types (centralized, decentralized, pooled, and reinsurance) stemming from a distinction between policy and polity support. In terms of the drivers of support and its evolution over time, performance evaluations and ideational factors appear as strong predictors, while perceived threat and economic vulnerability appear to matter less. Results show strong support for further resource pooling at the EU level in all domains that can lead to novel and differentiated forms of polity-building. This title is also available as Open Access on Cambridge Core.

Keywords: public opinion, state-building, polity formation, European integration, Ukraine

ISBNs: 9781009497602 (HB), 9781009497626 (PB), 9781009497596 (OC)
ISSNs: 2754-5032 (online), 2754-5024 (print)

Contents

1   Introduction   1

2   EU Polity Support – A Theoretical and Empirical
    Framework   7

3   Refugee Policy   27

4   Energy Policy   38

5   Foreign Policy   49

6   Military Policy   58

7   Conclusions   69

    References   78

An online appendix for this publication can be accessed at
www.cambridge.org/polity_building

1 Introduction

The Russian invasion of Ukraine came on the heels of a series of crises that tested the resilience of the EU as a compound polity (Ferrera, Kriesi, and Schelkle 2024). It has also, arguably, reshaped European policymaking at all levels and impacted the polity itself. This external threat triggered a debate between those arguing it can lead to an external security logic of polity building that serves as an impetus for (further) polity centralization in the EU, as per the 'bellicist' argument (e.g., Kelemen and McNamara 2021) and those who doubt it (e.g., Genschel and Schimmelfennig 2022). Taking the Russian invasion of Ukraine as a litmus test of the 'bellicist' argument, some contributions to the debate have questioned the extent to which it can really be conducive to polity centralization. The literature also casts some shadow of doubt on the extent to which such a threat is different than other threats and crises that the EU has been facing over the last couple of decades and the types of polity formation logics (external security vs. social security) it would trigger and their expected effects (Eilstrup-Sangiovanni 2022; Freudlsperger and Schimmelfennig 2022; Genschel and Schimmelfennig 2022; Ferrera and Schelkle 2024). Other contributions have explored specific topics such as the ways in which a rally around the European flag has evolved in the aftermath of the Russian invasion of Ukraine (Moise et al. 2023; Truchlewski, Oana, and Moise 2023), or the nature of public opinion surrounding specific policies (Moise, Dennison, and Kriesi 2023; Wang and Moise 2023; Oana, Moise, and Truchlewski 2024). More generally, this debate is crucial for understanding the political dynamics that shape the current pathways of European polity formation.

This Element expands this debate in several ways and offers an empirically grounded analysis of the effects that the Russian invasion of Ukraine had on public support for European polity building in key policy domains. Focusing on public opinion support is important given the politicization of the European polity (Kriesi, Hutter, and Grande 2016), the debates on the democratic deficit in the EU and the weakness of voice channels (Bartolini 2005), but also as a supportive public opinion offers an enabling environment for policymaking at the EU level and could take the wind out of Euroskeptic parties' sails. While this Element is definitely not the first to focus on public opinion in the EU in times of crises (De Vries 2018; Kriesi et al. 2024), it does bring in several theoretical and empirical contributions that offer unique analytical gains and novelty. These contributions are inspired by the polity approach to the European Union (Bartolini 2005; Ferrera 2005; Caramani 2015; Ferrera, Kriesi, and Schelkle 2024) arguing for the multi-dimensionality and lack of finalité in European integration. In other words, the building of the EU polity need not imply a full transfer or new creation of 'core' institutions to the EU at the expense of the Member States. Instead, this approach acknowledges there can be a variety of polity-building pathways if one looks at the constitute elements of the EU as a polity (Ladi and Wolff 2021; Ferrera, Kyriazi, and Miró 2024; Truchlewski et al. 2025).

First, in line with this approach, rather than conceiving of public support for the EU as uni-dimensional – more or less integration – we conceive of such support as playing out in two dimensions stemming from a distinction between 'policy' and 'polity' support. By *policy* support, we refer here to support for pooling decision-making and/or resources at the EU level in specific policy domains. By *polity* support, we refer to a general positive attitude to the EU based on a deeper loyalty towards the polity. In other words, policy support is analogous to specific support, while polity support is analogous to diffuse support for the EU (Easton 1975). While specific and diffuse EU support have been related to one another in previous studies, we argue that they do not necessarily always go together and that studying their intersections opens up a richer analytical space in which public support for the EU can be categorized into four types: support for a *centralized* polity (high loyalty and high preference for pooling), *decentralized* one (low loyalty and low preference for pooling), *pooled* polity (low loyalty but high preference for pooling), or a *reinsurance* polity (high loyalty but low preference for pooling).[1]

The second theoretical assumption that we start with is that crises are not monolithic threats. Crises play out in different policy domains and support for types of EU polity can vary across these domains as a function of the asymmetries that they exacerbate between countries and social groups, of the performance of European institutions and Member States in these crises, and/or of previous attitudes. These factors drive out territorial divisions – between citizens in different Member States – and functional divisions – between groups of citizens across Member States. In other words, akin to what the literature calls vertical differentiated integration (Holzinger and Schimmelfennig 2012; Dirk Leuffen and Díaz 2022; Schimmelfennig, Leuffen, and Vries 2023), support for the four polity types is policy domain-specific. This implies that there can be different polity-building pathways across policy domains, rather than a single logic of integration.

When it comes to the determinants of support for polity types across policy domains we, thus, inquire both into territorial divisions – *between* Member States – and into functional divisions – between social and attitudinal groups, *within* Member States. Concerning territorial divisions, we focus on the

---

[1] We develop the rationale for these four polity types in Section 2.

distribution of preferences for our four polity types between Member States and how these vary across policy domains. Concerning functional divisions, our manuscript brings together under the same umbrella three main sets of factors that have previously been associated with support for the EU. First, in line with the cleavage and post-functionalist literature (Vries and Edwards 2009; Hooghe and Marks 2018, 2009), we examine the relationship between ideational factors such as ideology and support for EU polity types. Second, going beyond deep-rooted attitudes, we also examine the relationship between crisis performance evaluations of both the EU and national governments as stemming out from the literature on output legitimacy (Scharpf 1999; Jones 2009; Schmidt 2013). Finally, in line with more recent literature on external drivers of EU support, we look at factors related to the 'bellicist' argument and the hard security logic of EU polity building such as threat perceptions stemming from the invasion (Genschel 2022; Kelemen and McNamara 2022; Truchlewski, Oana, and Moise 2023; Moise, Truchlewski, and Oana 2024), but also those related to a 'Milwardian' social security logic (Milward, Brennan, and Romero 1992; Natili and Visconti 2023; Ferrera and Schelkle 2024) such as economic vulnerability. This allows us to examine and compare under the same theoretical and empirical umbrella the impact of both internal and external drivers of demand for different types of polities.

Beyond theoretically expanding the debate on EU support in light of the Russian invasion of Ukraine, we also empirically ground it by mobilizing a host of original public opinion data. Our Element relies on cross-national survey data that we contextualize using secondary source analyses of policy- and polity-making decisions undertaken in the EU during the invasion. Our empirical focus on public opinion is theoretically justified as, in line with the postfunctionalist literature (Hooghe and Marks 2009), we consider this to be one of the key mechanisms in the long causal chain between threats and polity formation (Truchlewski, Oana, and Moise 2023). Public support for both policies, but also for the EU polity at large, has the potential to tie or free the hands of policymakers at both the Member State and the EU level. At the Member State level, domestic policymakers are aware of the electoral consequences of their decisions and attempt to satisfy public opinion at home when making decisions on the EU stage. At the EU level, European policymakers have an interest in polity maintenance (Ferrera, Miró, and Ronchi 2021; Ferrera, Kriesi, and Schelkle 2024) and avoiding backlashes from domestic audiences. Nevertheless, beyond public support, we acknowledge that the structure of the polity in terms of how strong or weak its subunits are, how centralized, and so on, is important in shaping policy and polity responses to (external) threats (Genschel 2022; Moise, Truchlewski, and Oana 2024). We take this into account both by the fact that we examine the Russian invasion of Ukraine not as a monolithic threat spurring just an external security logic of polity-building, but as a series of threats affecting various policy domains in which the EU and the Member States have different competence distributions and powers at the centre of the polity might differ, and by examining both policy and polity support. In sum, by contextualizing public opinion in various policy domains and under the various decisions undertaken in these domains during the invasion, we also inquire into the ways in which the structure of the polity itself is shaping public opinion support.

We further these empirical goals by using original public opinion data collected within the ERC Synergy project SOLID at three-time points (March, July, and December 2022) after the Russian invasion of Ukraine, forming an original three-wave panel in five countries (Germany, France, Italy, Hungary, and Poland) with an additional two countries (Finland and Portugal) studied only in the second wave. Panel data has the unique advantage of tracking individuals over time enabling an examination of how their attitudes shift in response to the changing conditions of the conflict. It also allows more in-depth exploration of the interplay between attitudes, such as crisis performance evaluations, and security conditions, such as vulnerabilities enhanced by the war. Our panel data, therefore, allows us to study the dynamics of EU public opinion through a critical juncture for EU policy and decision-making. The EU and its Member States are directly involved in the war, through refugee acceptance, sanctions, energy policy, military aid, humanitarian relief, and other geopolitical and national decisions. Russia itself claims that it is at war not just with Ukraine, but with the whole of NATO. European publics have, therefore, been exposed to a geopolitical struggle between the West and Russia, with the EU taking a strong role. They have been exposed to the quick, emergency-style, consensual policymaking of the beginning of the war, as well as to the later disagreements among member states over sanctions, energy policy, and grain exports. Respondents have been exposed to the terrifying images of war crimes and, particularly in Eastern countries, also to the threat of Russian aggression and possible escalation. Our period of study, therefore, captures what is, to date, the most salient external threat to the European polity. It is, therefore, the ideal scenario in which to test the 'bellicist' argument, starting from the demand side.

To sum up, our Element brings in several key contributions to the debate on EU polity building in the aftermath of the invasion:

- *First*, we seek to address the debate by delving deeper into the polity formation logics that are triggered across policy domains. Our Element pushes forward a distinction between 'policy' and 'polity' dynamics. By policy dynamics, we refer here to the specific support for decisions in various policy domains concerning the distribution of the burden of the shock across these policies among Member States. By polity dynamics, we refer to the shape and evolution of diffuse support for the EU based on a deeper loyalty towards the polity. By analogy, the polity is the container, while policies are what is contained. We argue that this distinction is important for capturing the various polity formation pathways upon which Europe can embark within crises. Rather than conceiving of public support for the EU as uni-dimensional – more or less integration – we conceive of such support as playing out in these two dimensions. Studying the intersections between these dimensions opens a richer analytical space for categorizing public support for the EU. We, hence, propose four polity types at the intersection of policy/specific and polity/diffuse support: a *centralized* polity (high loyalty and high preference for pooling), a *decentralized* one (low loyalty and low preference for pooling), a *pooled* polity (low loyalty but high preference for pooling), and a *reinsurance* polity (high loyalty but low preference for pooling).

- *Second*, in contrast to what has been labelled as the 'bellicist' argument, we argue that the Russian invasion of Ukraine exerted pressures on a variety of different policy domains with the potential to spur not only an external security logic of polity building (i.e., centralizing the defence domain as a consequence of the external threat) but also other logics of polity building such as a social security one – that is, centralizing of risk and redistribution in other policy domains to cope with the fallout of the crisis (Moise et al. 2023). In this Element, we further develop this idea that crises are not monolithic threats, but rather that they play out in different domains and support for EU polity types can vary across these as a function of the asymmetries that they exacerbate between countries and social groups. Consequently, the EU itself is not viewed as subject to more or less integration uniformly across the polity, but can be conceived of as an amalgamation of different polity types across policy domains. This idea structures the content of the Element as we analyse four highly salient policy domains on which the Russian invasion of Ukraine induced high pressures for reform – refugee policy, energy policy, foreign policy, and defence – while also focusing on the similarities and differences between them.
- *Third*, we contribute to the literature on the internal and external drivers of European polity formation and their relative weight. While the literature on European integration has classically been focused on internal drivers of polity formation, political economists have long been acquainted with the idea of the 'second image reversed' in international politics (Gourevitch 1978), that is, the idea that external crises affect domestic political cleavages and

thus shape the policy response and the development of any polity (Rogowski 1989; Midford 1993; Alt et al. 1996). The same is true of the Russian invasion of Ukraine and its influence on the formation of the European polity (Moise, Truchlewski, and Oana 2024). It is only recently that scholars started paying attention to the mechanism of external threats influencing the EU (Kelemen and McNamara 2022), leveraging an old literature on the sources of state-building and federalism (Riker 1964; Tilly 1975). We compare the impact of internal and external drivers of demand for different types of polities.

- *Fourth*, our Element attempts to further empirically ground the debate surrounding the polity formation consequences of the Russian invasion of Ukraine. In doing so, we critically focus on public opinion as an important link in the chain of polity formation given the politicization of the European polity, criticism of democratic deficit in the EU and of weak voice channels, but also as a supportive public opinion offer an enabling environment for policymaking at the EU level. In light of this, the Russian Invasion of Ukraine and its impact on the European polity offers a critical case study of the linkage between public opinion and polity formation. Empirically, we use a host of original public opinion data consisting of a unique three-wave panel survey on the topic of EU polity building following the invasion.

Across the four empirical sections, we show that all four polity types that we conceptualize at the intersections between policy and polity attitudes (centralized, decentralized, pooled, and reinsurance) are supported by large percentages of European publics. These results illustrate that two categories of citizens that are largely ignored in studies of EU support, those who want to centralize decisions in particular domains but have low loyalty towards the polity and those who, while having high loyalty, still do not want to centralize, constitute significant groups across all of our policy domains. In terms of the determinants of EU support, we show that performance evaluations and ideational factors are significantly related to preferences for polity types across all four domains, while external factors such as perceived threats and economic vulnerability stemming from the invasion have a lower impact. These results hold not only when examining static relations between these attitudes but also when examining within-individual change across the crisis. Hence, preferences for our four polity types are more strongly rooted in output legitimacy and deep attitudinal variables, rather than in factors directly related to the security or economic threats raised by the war. Beyond these attitudinal divisions, our results also show important territorial divisions between citizens in different Member States, divisions which vary greatly across policy domains.

While countries are hardly divided over refugee policy (with the exception of Hungary), across the other three policy fields studied in the manuscript we observe varying potential 'coalitions' of citizens across Member States likely as a consequence of the asymmetrical impact of the crisis.

The Element proceeds as follows. Section 2 sets the scene by introducing the theoretical framework and the empirical design. Sections 3–7 examine EU support across the four policy domains chosen: refugee policy (Section 3), energy policy (Section 4), foreign policy (Section 5), and defence (Section 6). Each of these empirical sections starts with a descriptive analysis of support for the four polity types that we introduce in our theoretical section. It then analyses statically the territorial divisions in such support and the relationship between individual factors related to performance evaluations, ideational factors, and security factors. Finally, each empirical section includes a dynamic analysis of within-individual attitudinal changes over time. The Element ends with a concluding section where we summarize our theoretical contributions as well as our empirical findings and discuss their wider implications.

2 EU Polity Support – A Theoretical and Empirical Framework

This section lays out the theoretical and empirical design of our Element. We begin by justifying our focus on public opinion, emphasizing its critical role in the context of the increasing politicization of the European polity and its influence as an enabler of European policymaking. We then focus on the conceptualization of the demand-side support for EU polity building in times of crises, putting forward two significant contributions inspired by the polity formation approach to the European Union (Caramani 2015; Ferrera, Kriesi, and Schelkle 2024). First, in line with this approach arguing for the absence of a clear *finalité* in the process of European integration, we say that the building of the EU polity does not necessarily imply a full transfer of sovereignty or the creation of 'core state power' institutions at the EU level. By contrast, there can be a variety of polity-building pathways that need not imply centralization at the EU level (Ladi and Wolff 2021; Ferrera, Kyriazi, and Miró 2024; Truchlewski et al. 2025). We leverage this insight and propose a four-fold typology of support for the EU polity stemming from a distinction between polity and policy attitudes. Second, we argue that crises are not monolithic threats but that they instead exacerbate divisions between Member States (territorial) and social groups (functional) that vary across policy domains. In light of this, we introduce the policy domains that this Element focuses on and theorize the kinds of divisions that are likely to be associated with polity support across these domains. When discussing these divisions and the drivers of EU policy support we bring under the same theoretical and empirical umbrella both internal – such as output legitimacy and ideology – and external – such as threat perceptions – factors influencing support. Finally, we conclude the section by briefly introducing our data and the design of the empirical analyses.

2.1 Public Opinion and the EU Polity Formation

Since 1992, the politicization of European polity formation has brought public opinion into the picture of European politics (Hooghe and Marks 2009). The 1992 referendum failure in Denmark, which rejected the Maastricht Treaty, and the reluctant 'little yes' uttered by French voters marked the end of the permissive consensus and elite-driven European polity formation. More than ever after a decade-plus of crises, the EU relies on different types of support from electorates. Polity building – as embodied by the many reforms and capacity building at the centre – needs to be fully supported by voters to be sustainable in the long run and not exploited by euro-skeptic party actors. We, thus, argue that mapping out potential conflicts – whether functional or territorial (Caramani 2015) – is vital for understanding where political frictions can appear and how they will influence the future of both European polity formation and the Russian invasion of Ukraine (since Ukraine relies on its European allies for crucial help).

While the argument of external threats inducing polity centralization that stems from the state-building literature (Riker 1964; Hintze 1975; Tilly 1975; Kelemen and McNamara 2021) has been chiefly focused on the supply side of politics (policymakers) and does not have much to say about public demand for polity centralization, we argue that the demand side is an important link in the chain going from the external threat to polity centralization (Truchlewski, Oana, and Moise 2023).

First, the Hintze–Riker–Tilly thesis was developed to explain state formation in the Middle Ages and the Renaissance when elites operated without much popular constrain and when military technology required economies of scale that needed to go beyond the feudal structure (Cederman et al. 2023). Modern democratic nation-states need to consider public opinion, as it may constrain or enable elite action. We know that a strong dissensus among the European public can constrain further political integration (Hooghe and Marks 2009). Conversely, a strong consensus allows greater room of manoeuvre for politicians to steer the shape of the EU polity. At the Member State level, domestic policymakers are aware of the electoral consequences of their decisions and attempt to satisfy public opinion at home when making decisions on the EU stage. At the EU level, European policymakers have an interest in polity maintenance and, hence, avoiding backlashes from domestic audiences that could threaten the polity and bring about divisions that would undermine common decision-making (Ferrera, Miró, and Ronchi 2021; Ferrera, Kriesi, and Schelkle 2024).

Furthermore, we note that public opinion is more likely to exert pressure on politicians during times of high salience when voters follow what is happening and have more well-formed preferences. The present moment is, therefore, an opportunity to probe into demand-side dynamics at a time when the public is particularly attuned to the Russian invasion of Ukraine and the response of the EU. [2] We started our panel survey at the onset of the invasion in 2022, a moment of very high salience for the Russian war in Ukraine and the economic and political response of the EU. Thus, while several of the policy domains associated with the invasion (foreign policy, energy, etc.) are usually considered too complex for individuals and of low salience, our timing allows us to examine them in a situation when the public is aware and engaged in discussions surrounding the implications of these policies. Indeed, several elections, such as those in Hungary[3] and Slovakia,[4] showed that policies concerning the war were crucial for electoral success. All in all, we argue that in case of an external threat, when highly salient policies take centre stage in the public sphere, consensus on the demand side becomes crucial for policymaking.

Second, and more generally, following the polity approach to the European Union (Bartolini 2005; Ferrera, Kriesi, and Schelkle 2024) that draws on the Hirschman-Rokkan model of state-building (Hirschman 1970; Rokkan et al. 1999), we look at bonding as one of the main elements characterizing a polity (alongside bounding–borders and binding–authority/capacity).[5] Bonding refers to the loyalty and solidarity that members of a polity have towards the polity itself and towards other members, a loyalty that ultimately constitutes

---

[2] When asked in our survey, 32 per cent of respondents thought that the war in Ukraine was the most important threat to the survival of the EU, with a further 21 per cent citing it as the second most significant threat. Other option categories included climate change, financial crises, refugee inflows from outside Europe, refugee inflows from within Europe, member states leaving the EU, poverty and unemployment, and pandemics.

[3] www.bbc.com/news/world-europe-60977917.

[4] www.ft.com/content/9de49e7a-d830-4d5d-8615-2c00ba6f8552 and https://www.ft.com/content/4bd9bd86-69bb-40a1-8570-e40930208300.

[5] The relationship between these three elements is one of the main arguments in Rokkanian theory which suggests that external closure – strong borders would produce further political structuring – capacity and system building – loyalty. Others (Ferrera, Kriesi, and Schelkle 2024; Truchlewski et al. 2025) have argued for other configurations and re-configurations between these three elements. While we consider this an important topic of investigation, it is one that goes beyond the scope of this Element which focuses mainly on bonding at the demand-side level.

the political community (Oana and Truchlewski 2024). Investigating how thin or volatile such bonding is in times of crises on the demand side is important as it speaks not only to the amount of resistance there is in the EU against pooling resources and decisions in particular policy domains but also to the potential for triggering more foundational conflicts over the *raison d'être* of the polity itself (Ferrera, Kriesi, and Schelkle 2024).

Nevertheless, we do not yet have a good understanding of how the demand side of politics is affected by external threats and by the Russian invasion of Ukraine in particular. The evidence so far shows that similarly to the COVID pandemic (Altiparmakis et al. 2021; Beetsma, Burgoon, and Nicoli 2023; Bremer et al. 2023), the Russian invasion of Ukraine triggered a rally-round-the-flag moment among European voters, who became more supportive of leaders and policies following the start of the war (Steiner et al. 2023; Truchlewski, Oana, and Moise 2023; Nicoli et al. 2024). Importantly, this implies that EU elites have greater room for manoeuvring in order to pursue certain forms of polity building. Conversely, if far-right parties are not able to capitalize on possible dissensions, they may prove unable to create political momentum against policies and polity formation, as postfunctionalism would predict (Hooghe and Marks 2009). However, as we further argue in the next section, such a rally-round-the-flag is likely to vary across policy domains. Furthermore, support might be short-lived and give way to more dissensus as the crisis progresses. By focusing on the demand side of politics, our manuscript aims to shed light on these developments.

2.2 Beyond Integration: Conceptualizing Polity Support across Policy Domains

We argued that analyzing the demand side of EU politics in the aftermath of the Russian invasion of Ukraine is important given the war's public salience and given public opinion's crucial role in enabling or constraining policymaking. While this Element is definitely not the first to focus on public opinion in the EU in times of crises (De Vries 2018; Kriesi et al. 2024; Truchlewski et al. 2025), it does start from two consequential theoretical assumptions inspired by the polity approach to the European Union (Caramani 2015; Ferrera, Kriesi, and Schelkle 2024) that bring about unique analytical gains and novelty. First, rather than considering public support for the EU as uni-dimensional – more or less integration, we conceive of such support as playing out in two dimensions stemming from a distinction between 'policy' and 'polity' support. Second, we argue that crises are not monolithic threats but that they play out in different policy domains, and support for types of EU polity can vary across these domains. In this section, we elaborate on both of these arguments.

2.2.1 A Typology of Public Support for the EU

Europe is at a crossroads: repeated crises are reshaping it since the mid 2000s, oftentimes in counter-intuitive ways. Most surprising perhaps is an outcome that did not happen: contrary to what many established theories predicted and in spite of what many politicians and analysts wish, Europe did not 'integrate' uniformly across policy fields into a fully-fledged federation (Tilly 1990; Kelemen and McNamara 2021). Nor did the EU disintegrate and decentralize policy fields after massive policy failures (Vollaard 2014; Leruth, Gänzle, and Trondal 2019). Rather, new forms of collective policymaking appeared following the tectonic pressures of various crises: for instance, the EU started elaborating a 'reinsurance regime' (Schelkle 2014, 2017, 2022, 2023a, 2023b; Truchlewski et al. 2025) where the EU acts as a backstop of last resort for European member states. European capacity building is comparatively thin, and its main purpose is to 'rescue the nation-state', as Milward famously put it. Other forms of (un-)intended collective policymaking have been theorized (e.g., 'extensive unification' - Ferrera, Kyriazi, and Miró 2024; Truchlewski et al., 2025 or 'coordinative Europeanization' - Ladi and Wolff, 2021), and the main message is that we need an approach that captures them. These unintended outcomes of European polity formation in hard times underline that polities can form along different pathways – from centralized nation-states to federations and confederations, to name but a few (Stepan 1999). While the unintended consequences argument ('spillovers') has always been a key argument of neofunctionalist theories of European integration (Haas 1958), the neofunctionalists also stress the idea of a general upward trend towards further integration which crises might just delay (Hooghe and Marks 2019). By contrast, the polity approach, resting on a historical-institutional argument, stresses the importance of not just path dependence, but also critical junctures such as crises, which open the door for different polity formation pathways (Pierson 1996). Finally, and since the EU is also a democratic polity, public opinion plays a crucial role in shaping which polity pathways will be taken: this is because public opinion constrains decision-makers and sets the parameters not only of the possible but also of the probable (Hooghe and Marks 2009).

When it comes to Europe, however, the probable is too often reduced to a binary choice. Policy-makers and their electorate may choose either more or less integration. The postfunctionalist literature (Hooghe and Marks 2009, 2018), while informative in bringing a demand-side focus in the study of European integration, also tends to model support for or against Europe in an uni-dimensional fashion (more or less integration) which we argue that does fully cover the multi-dimensionality that public preferences surrounding the

EU can take. The same problem belies the state formation literature which more often than not assumes that in times of crisis, only one logic dominates polity building: the external security logic (Tilly 1985, 1990; Kelemen and McNamara 2021), that is, the need to centralize coercive means at the centre of the polity to reap the benefits of economies of scale, organized communication and centralized command-and-control. Consequently, citizens can mostly express feelings towards more or less centralization. Such binary choices, we argue, do not reflect wide possibilities of what are probable polity formation pathways. For instance, Europeans can decide to pool decision-making processes, but not necessarily their material capacities. A case in point is the push for greater majority voting in the Council whilst leaving material levers of action at the national level. We argue that capturing such polity pathways is best addressed not only by asking whether citizens want more or less integration but rather by inquiring into what type of integration they want.

Other recent contributions to the study of EU support have also taken stock of the insight concerning the multi-dimensionality of support (for instance Boomgaarden et al. 2011; Anderson and Hecht 2018; Leuffen, Schuessler, and Gómez Díaz 2022; Schüssler et al. 2023 and in particular De Vries 2018). In line with this insight, to avoid conceptual ambiguities, we propose to expand the analytical space that captures the various pathways that Europe can embark on when crises force decisions and reforms. Thus, rather than conceptualizing public support for the EU as uni-dimensional – more or less integration – we conceive of such support as playing out in two dimensions stemming from a distinction between 'policy' and 'polity' support. This distinction is based on the classic differentiation between specific (policy) and diffuse (polity) support (Easton 1975). In line with this, support can be both specific for certain policies and diffuse for the polity itself more generally. The policy dimension, akin to specific support, refers to domain-specific attitudes related to the pooling of resources and/or decisions through different mechanisms like centralization or coordination to share the burden in a particular domain. In other words, this relates to what is 'contained' within the polity, that is, how much decisions and/or capacities are pooled in the centre of the EU. The polity dimension, akin to diffuse support, refers to attitudes related to a deeper loyalty towards the polity. These attitudes relate to the 'container' – the polity itself. Recent literature has highlighted that support for policies – the contained – is also conditional on their institutional design – the container (Burgoon et al. 2022; Bremer et al. 2023; Beetsma, Burgoon, and Nicoli 2023; Ferrara, Schelkle, and Truchlewski 2023; Nicoli, Duin, and Burgoon 2023; Blok et al. 2024). Hence, we investigate such specific and diffuse types of support by looking at support for, respectively, European policies and the European polity itself.

Table 1 Pathways of EU polity formation

Pathways of EU polity formation		Polity	
		Partially/Not loyal	**More/Fully loyal**
Policy	More/Full centralization	*Pooled*	*Centralized*
	Partial/No centralization	*Decentralized*	*Reinsurance*

While specific and diffuse EU support have been related to one another in previous studies, we argue that they need not always correlate and that their intersections open a richer analytical space in which public support for the EU can be categorized. Hence, we propose a two-by-two typology (see Table 1) that categorizes support for the EU into four possible polity types: support for a centralized polity, a decentralized one, a pooled polity, or a reinsurance polity. While the concept of European integration only captures the first two of these and conflates the other categories into one of these extremes, we show across the four empirical sections that all four of these categories are supported by large percentages of European public and a sizable share of respondents locate themselves in the pooled and reinsurance types of polities. Note that these categories are ideal types that need not represent the status-quo in specific policy fields. The three categories are forward-looking and akin to ideal types: they signify preferences for possible polity formation pathways, rather than represent the status-quo in these specific policy areas. We argue that this typology gives us a much more fine-grained conceptual apparatus to empirically engage with support for the EU and to map theoretically richer possible outcomes.

The first possible type of EU support and polity formation pathway is that of a *centralized* polity. Citizens preferring this type of polity not only have a high loyalty towards the polity (e.g., high diffuse and general preferences for integration) but also want means/structures to be centralized in particular policy domains. By contrast, at the opposite end of the spectrum, we have citizens who prefer a *decentralized* polity. These citizens have low loyalty towards the polity and do not want to centralize means or structures. The first of the new categories that our typology brings in is that of the *pooled* polity. Citizens preferring such a polity have low loyalty towards the polity but want centralization in particular policy domains. Citizens in this category might want to pragmatically pool resources to face a shock, especially when subunits might have weak 'infrastructural capacity' (Mann 2012; Genschel and Jachtenfuchs 2014). Finally, the other new category that our typology brings in is that of the *reinsurance* polity in which high loyalty is coupled with low preferences for pooling means or structures in particular policy domains (Schelkle 2017, 2022, 2023a, 2023b). This category draws from the idea that strong loyalty does not necessarily imply preferences for further capacity building. In general, it is not a foregone conclusion that subunits will pool resources: if the subunits have a strong 'infrastructural capacity', they will be reluctant to pool resources because the opportunity cost of doing so is losing political control (vs. creating new ex nihilo resources at the centre does not have this opportunity cost).

The two new categories that our typology introduces, pooled and reinsurance, also speak to competence and control theories of indirect governance (Genschel and Jachtenfuchs 2013; Abbott et al. 2020). These theories highlight the idea that any problem of governance is under-girded by principal-agent dynamics: principals face a dilemma between delegating to agents for more efficient action (competence) and controlling these agents so that they fulfil the task they are assigned to and do not exploit information asymmetries to pursue their own goal (control). In any polity, delegating competence without control can be politically perilous. Conversely, too much control over delegated competence can stifle efficiency. The problem of control also refers to the need for polity centralization: for any collective action to be efficient, agents also need to impose control so that principals do not renege on their initial commitment to common problem-solving. Hence, the need for common rules and institutions that enforce them.

Analogously, we could say that the pooled polity type stresses competence over control. In other words, supporters of the pooled polity type are pragmatists in that they want efficient solutions to policy-specific problems even if these solutions might imply the pooling of means away from principals – in the EU polity these would be the Member States. By contrast, the reinsurance type stresses control over competence: supporters of this type want control at the centre of the polity but with competencies remaining in the hands of the principals. Hence, our reinsurance type is akin to the regulatory polity stressing integration by regulation (Genschel and Jachtenfuchs 2013) as core-state powers (and pooling of means) would remain firmly at the member-state level, but the EU would have regulatory control over these powers and a capacity to support member states when these cannot cope with extraordinary events (Schelkle 2014, 2023b). However, while in these theories integration by regulation is opposed to integration by capacity building – integration that puts the EU on the pathway to state-building, our typology stresses that capacity building or the pooling of means can also be further differentiated. While a centralized polity would indeed imply capacity building but one that is placed on a firm basis of loyalty and with increased control and permanence at the centre, the pooled category refers to more pragmatic forms of centralization across policy domains that do not necessarily imply a mustering of core-state powers and needn't be permanent.

A final note is worth mentioning related to the variation possible between the polity types within and across policy domains, but also across time. Polity-diffuse support is not policy domain-specific and hence does not vary across these domains, while policy support related to the decisions to centralize and pool resources are domain-specific. This implies that *within* each policy domain the four cells in our category can be of varying sizes, but when comparing *between* policy domains the size of the various support groups changes across vertical lines (from pooled to decentralized, or from centralized to reinsurance) in our Table 1 with the horizontal divisions in polity remaining stable across domains (i.e., the sum of the non-loyal group, with pooled and decentralized together staying constant across domains). Nevertheless, regarding variations over time, both vertical and horizontal variations are possible. Concerning the latter, polity attitudes can also change through time: as the crises progress, citizens' loyalty to the polity might, for example, increase, and they could move from the pooled type to the centralized type, or from the decentralized type to the reinsurance type. As the forthcoming sections show, all these types of movements are observed empirically.

2.2.2 Public Support for the EU across Policy Domains

Our second contribution is to show that this four-fold analytical space applies to different degrees to different key policies. We argue that crises like the Russian war in Ukraine are not monolithic threats, but they operate through different channels of policy and polity preferences. In line with this, the external security logic can be complemented by other logics of polity formation kicking in: the social security logic (Moise et al. 2023), that is, the need for every polity and polity response to be focused on redistribution and sustaining prosperity or, for instance, the legal logic of polity formation (Strayer 1970; Kelemen 2011; Pavone 2022) through the emergence of an autonomous legal order. Accordingly, pooling means and structures may more or less be supported in some policy domains that others, which again underscores the idea that European integration is not a one-way street in the citizens' mind, but rather a plurality of possible paths along which a polity can be build which can unfold differently in different policies.

Studying preferences for these polity formation pathways is particularly relevant in the context of the Russian invasion of Ukraine not only as one of the likely cases in which demands for centralization or pooling can increase, according to the bellicist argument, but also as the threat coming from the invasion is multi-faceted and can highlight specific policy vulnerabilities in a polity (Moise et al. 2024). Hence, contrary to the bellicist argument focused on defence centralization, we argue that the threats of the invasion play out in different policy domains and support four types of EU polity that can vary across these domains as a function of the asymmetries that they exacerbate between countries and social groups, the performance of European and Member state actors, or of previous attitudes. These factors drive out territorial divisions – between citizens in different Member States and functional divisions – between groups of citizens across Member States.

We select four key policy domains of high salience in the crisis: refugee, energy, foreign policy, and defence. These policy fields represent the main vulnerabilities of the EU polity in this crisis and are subject to varying degrees of division between and within Member States.

The influx of refugees is a direct result of the war, and refugee policy is one of the main vulnerabilities that the conflict exacerbates. Between Member States, the pressures coming from the refugee influx are highly asymmetric with some countries, such as Poland and Germany, receiving the bulk of Ukrainian refugees. Within Member States, refugee policy and burden-sharing are some of the most politicized issues by far-right parties. Such territorial and functional divisions stood behind the intense conflict and eventual stop-gap, externalization solution of the 2015 refugee crisis (Kriesi et al. 2024). Nevertheless, existing evidence suggests that in spite of these asymmetries, there is strong support for burden-sharing both between Member States and socio-political groups (Moise, Dennison, and Kriesi 2023).

Energy policy was directly weaponized by Russia as a way of punishing the EU for its support of Ukraine, and to fight back against other sanctions which could spur unity. Nevertheless, the energy threat induced by the crisis and the rising energy costs stemming from the energy transition are being experienced asymmetrically both between member states (given differences in energy dependence and geopolitical context), and within member states (due to various individual preferences and vulnerabilities) (Oana, Moise, and Truchlewski 2024). Such asymmetries can exacerbate transnational and domestic conflicts and can thus undermine common EU decision-making and solidarity.

The foreign policy of the EU is both a source of strength and weakness for the EU polity: due to the structure of its decision-making based on consensus and vetoes, the EU can either manage to speak with one voice – which makes it appear as united and strong – or can quickly descend into paralysis as even the smallest of its Member States can veto decisions. This problem is exacerbated by the fact that foreign policy is a domain in which economies of scale are much less tangible than in material policies like defence or energy. As a consequence of this, there is a high likelihood that Member States might wish to maintain autonomy and sovereignty. Furthermore, geopolitical factors such as proximity to the conflict zone might further exacerbate this problem: countries bordering a crisis-prone region may want to upload their policy solution to the whole polity, while countries far away may be reluctant to share the cost of a problem that is not theirs.

Finally, studying the defence domain is particularly important for studying the bellicist logic of polity formation: the threat stemming from the Russian invasion of Ukraine should result in more demand for centralization in the realm of defence. Nevertheless, this policy domain is characterized not only by the strength of the sub-units (Member States have highly developed national armies), but also by the external security guarantee provided by NATO both factors which might reduce the impetus for pooling and centralizing defence resources (Moise, Truchlewski, and Oana 2024). Furthermore, arming Ukraine is already highlighting tensions between member states over which weapons to send and how to reimburse other member states.

2.3 The Drivers of Support for EU Polity Types

The literature on public support for the European polity has already theorized its different potential drivers. Our aim in this manuscript is to bring them under the same comparative umbrella and analyse their relationship with our proposed measure of EU polity support across policy domains. In line with Caramani 2015 (but also more recent contributions to the literature on EU support or solidarity, Kriesi, Moise, and Oana 2024; Oana and Truchlewski 2024; Truchlewski, Oana, and Natili 2024) which points out to the importance of two types of cleavages when it comes to the EU: territorial cleavages between the Member States and functional cleavages which are transnational and cut across territorial lines, we also look at both types of factors throughout our analyses. With regards to territorial cleavages, we examine divisions in public support across Member States and how these vary across policy domains. In what regards functional divisions we examine the extent to which preexisting and deep-seated predispositions and attitudes such as ideology are related to EU polity support, but also look at the effect of crisis or policy-specific factors on such support. We focus on two such crisis or policy-specific factors which are rarely discussed under the same umbrella: output legitimacy (Scharpf 1999; Jones 2009; Schmidt 2013), and security logics (Kelemen and McNamara 2022; Natili and Visconti 2023; Ferrera and Schelkle 2024) which have been put forward by various strands of literature on European polity formation. First, our framework integrating both territorial and functional divides speaks to the extent to which territoriality is dissipated within the EU across policy domain or replaced by cleavages cutting across these territories (Caramani 2015) as well as to the ways in which territorial and (post-)functional constraints could be re-enhanced, overcame, or bypassed altogether. Second, while the literature on European integration has classically been focused on internal drivers of polity formation, more recently scholars started paying attention to the mechanism of external threats influencing the EU (Kelemen and McNamara 2021). Our framework aims to bring together and compare the impact of both internal and external drivers of demand for different polity types.

2.3.1 Territorial Divisions

A large part of the literature on support for European integration emphasizes territorial divisions between Member States and the ways in which such divisions can slow down or paralyze policymaking by giving rise to divergent territorial coalitions that make agreeing to common solutions harder. This literature argues that the asymmetries that crises create between Member States given their various vulnerabilities, the wider political and socio-economic national context in which citizens live, and the positions of their national governments structure their preferences (Ferrara and Kriesi 2021). The crisis-focused literature has emphasized various transnational coalitions between member states in intergovernmental negotiations (Buti and Fabbrini 2022; Fabbrini 2022; Porte and Jensen 2022). For example, in the Euro-Area crisis, the literature has pointed to divisions between creditor and debtor countries or 'Northern Saints' and 'Southern Sinners' (Matthijs and McNamara 2015). In the refugee crisis, Kriesi et al. (2024) talk about a division between front-line states and open destination states (those receiving the bulk of refugees) and transit and closed destination states. In the COVID crisis, the literature (Kriesi, Moise, and Oana 2024; Truchlewski et al. 2025; Fabbrini 2022) highlights three main coalitions with divergent preferences: the 'Frugal 4' member states
(Austria, Denmark, the Netherlands, and Sweden), the 'solidaristic' Southern countries (Greece, Italy, Portugal, Spain, and one may add France), and the Visegrad four countries (Czech Republic, Hungary, Poland, and Slovakia). More recent studies (Kriesi, Moise, and Oana 2024) have shown that these transnational coalitions also play a role in the Ukraine crisis. In line with this and also starting from the assumption that such coalitions are also present in the aftermath of the invasion we examine territorial divisions between citizens in different Member States. We expect such divisions to matter, but we also expect them to vary across policy domains as a function of the Member State vulnerabilities that the crisis accentuates. We put forward our expectations in terms of the territorial divisions we foresee between these

(or other) coalitions of member states in each particular policy domain in the respective empirical sections.

2.3.2 Functional Divisions

Ideational Factors

The second strand of theories explaining the demand for EU integration also uses cleavage theory (Lipset and Rokkan 1967). This strand of theories argues that long-term social transformations are reshaping the structure of divides across the EU from territorial to functional divides that cross-cut across geography (Caramani 2015). This approach relates attitudes towards the European Union first and foremost to political ideology (Vries and Edwards 2009; Hooghe and Marks 2018; Hix and Høyland 2024). While some showcase the relationship between ideology and support for the EU as a U-shaped curve with those individuals that place themselves towards the centre of the left-right scale being more supportive of the EU than those that place themselves towards the extremes (Hooghe and Marks 2018), others (Hix and Høyland 2024) find that this relationship has changed dramatically over time as in the early years of European integration the right was more supportive of the EU, with this pattern reversing drastically after the 2000s. Generally, what the literature has in common is suggesting that the far-right has always been and still is associated with less support for the EU. Starting from this insight, we also expect that those citizens placing themselves towards the far right of the ideological scale would be less in favour of the three polity types that imply either high loyalty or pooling (centralized, pooled, and reinsurance) and more in favour of the decentralized polity type.

Output Legitimacy

Territorial and ideational explanations are usually robust indicators of EU support. However, given that territorial identities and ideology are rather stable as the result of deep-seated psychological predispositions they are expected to hardly change across policy domains or through time (Hooghe and Wilkenfeld 2008). By contrast, crisis and policy-specific factors can help us shed further light on such variation. The first set of such crisis/policy-specific factors that we look at are related to the discussion surrounding the criteria by which to evaluate the legitimacy of the EU. One such criterion that has been put forward in the previous literature is output legitimacy, and it refers to the effectiveness of the EU's policy outcomes for the people (Scharpf 1999; Jones 2009; Schmidt 2013). In line with this literature, we argue that citizens' satisfaction with the management of a crisis and its results has a likely impact on their support for specific polity types. We, hence, expect that the perceived efficiency or inefficiency of the EU in managing the crisis should have an impact specifically on preferences for pooling. In other words, the more citizens are dissatisfied with the performance of the EU in a particular polity domain the less they prefer the centralized and the pooled polity type. We expect this argument to also hold through time: changes in how satisfied an individual is would be strongly related to changes in polity type preferences as the crisis progresses.

Furthermore, keeping in mind the multilevel structure of the EU polity and its strong sub-units, we also expect the performance of national governments in the crisis to impact polity preferences. This insight is based on the 'benchmark' theory that contends that EU support does not develop in a vacuum and citizens' attitudes towards the EU are not only a result of how the EU itself performs but also a result of a comparison between national and EU evaluations (De Vries 2018). In our case, if the strong polity sub-units, that is, the Member States, are already perceived as fairing well in dealing with the crisis this reduces the need for pooling. Hence, the more satisfied one is with the performance of their government in dealing with a particular aspect of the crisis, the less one would prefer pooling in that particular policy domain.

Security Logics

While the literature on European integration has classically been focused on internal drivers of polity formation (i.e., ideational and output legitimacy), it is only more recently that scholars started paying attention to the mechanism of external threats influencing the EU (Kelemen and McNamara 2022), leveraging an old literature on the sources of state-building and federalism (Riker 1964; Tilly 1975). This 'bellicist' argument arguing that external security constitutes a strong driver for polity formation and centralization is generally focused on the supply side of politics. By contrast, we have argued that in the current era of mass democracy, a strong dissensus or consensus among European publics can constrain or enable policymaking (Hooghe and Marks 2009). In line with this, more recent literature has attempted to translate the 'bellicist' argument to the demand side of politics (Genschel 2022; Truchlewski, Oana, and Moise 2023; Moise, Truchlewski, and Oana 2024). This literature suggests that security concerns may prompt citizens in different member states to close ranks and demand more EU polity building. Indeed, studies of political behaviour show that exceptional circumstances and major crises (Mueller 1970, 1973; Altiparmakis et al. 2021; Bol et al. 2021; Schraff 2021; Steiner et al. 2023) give rise to moments of unity in which a majority of citizens show increased levels of political support. In other words, the perceived threat that a crisis poses can produce a rally-round-the-flag effect on the demand side, which would increase support for the EU. Following this strand of literature, we also use a measure of threat induced by the invasion and expect that the higher such threat, the stronger the preferences for pooling, that is, the higher the support for the centralized and pooled polity types.

However, while 'bellicist' theories focus on the impact of hard security threats on EU supports, others instead emphasize how the quest for social security is a strong driver of EU polity formation (Ferrera and Schelkle 2024). This argument aligns with a 'Milwardian' (Milward, Brennan, and Romero 1992) view of EU polity formation indicating that in compound polities, since the sub-units are states with considerable capacity in core state powers (Genschel and Jachtenfuchs 2014), instead of a transfer of such powers to the centre what is expected is for the EU to act as a safety net of the Member States. Because of this centralized European polity formation is expected to be predominantly achieved in the economic field. In line with this argument, on the demand side, it is actually citizens' demands for protection against social and economic risks that would increase their demand for the EU (Natili and Visconti 2023). Following the argument of the social security logic of EU polity building, we would expect that the economic vulnerabilities stemming from the invasion push citizens' preference for pooling resources at the EU level.

2.4 Design of the Study

2.4.1 Data

We further our empirical goals by using original public opinion data collected within the ERC Synergy project SOLID at three-time points (March, July, and December 2022) after the Russian invasion of Ukraine, forming an original three-wave panel in five countries: Germany, France, Italy, Hungary, and Poland. The second wave of our panel also included respondents from Finland and Portugal. The selection was these countries was guided by the idea of obtaining a wide amount of country heterogeneity in terms of reliance on Russian gas, political discourse related to sanctions, centrality in the EU, and geopolitical location that allows us to map preferences in a wide range of contexts. As further detailed in what follows, when comparing our data with other data sources with a wider geographical coverage on particular items of interest, the selected countries are fairly representative of wider European trends. Interviews were administered on national samples obtained using a quota design based on gender, age, macro-area of residence (NUTS-1), and education. Our total sample size is approximately 33,000 observations, while our panel respondents include 6,000 individuals surveyed over all three waves.

The first wave was carried out between 11 March and 5 April 2022, two weeks after the start of the war. This period captures attitudes at the very start of the war when the conflict dominated media channels across Europe, and thus the initial rally-around-the-flag effect (Truchlewski, Oana, and Moise 2023). EU member states came together in an unprecedented manner to form a common front against Russian aggression, applying sanctions, receiving refugees, and providing support to Ukraine. Attitudes from this period also tell us whether the EU may have missed a critical juncture for policy and polity change if such attitudes did not last. The second wave of our panel was conducted between 8 and 28 July 2022. Five months into the war saw a large decrease in salience, as other topics, including inflation and a looming energy crisis, took centre stage. At the same time, the conflict appeared in stale-mate after the spring, when the Ukrainians pushed Russian forces out from the capital, and the fighting concentrated on the South and East. The third wave was administered between 14 December 2022 and 4 January 2023. In between the second and third waves, the Ukrainian army made significant gains in the fall of 2022, showing the importance of Western-provided weapons and support. The timing of our third wave captured a period of calm in the conflict, while EU decision-making was focused primarily on energy policy and rising inflation.

While we focus on seven key member states over a roughly ten-month time-period following the start of the war, our findings speak to broader cross-country and over-time trends. Figure 1 shows how support for an integrated EU army fluctuates from 2018 to 2024 in fourteen EU countries.[6] What can be seen is that the war is a clear critical juncture, drastically shifting support in most countries starting in 2022, as already noted in the literature (Genschel 2022; Truchlewski, Oana, and Moise 2023). We see three types of countries. In France, Germany, Poland, and the Netherlands, we see stable support across time. In Denmark, Finland, Lithuania, Spain, Sweden, and the United Kingdom, we see strongly increased support in 2022, following the invasion, with some reversion in 2023–2024, but overall higher support. Lastly, in Italy, Hungary, and Romania, we see a decrease in support following the Russian invasion. Our sample of seven includes countries from each category, allowing us to study these dynamics in depth. Our analysis confirms the pattern of increasing initial support, followed by a slight reversion and then stability in

---

[6] Data come from the yearly administered EUI-Yougov solidarity survey (Hemerijck et al. 2022). The 2022 wave was conducted in April 2022, after the start of the war. Appendix Figure 7.2 presents the same data, including Bulgaria, Slovakia, and Croatia that only had data starting in 2022. Appendix Figure 7.3 shows the time trend for attitudes towards increasing defence against Russia, while Appendix Figure 7.4 shows support for other EU countries in case of military attack.

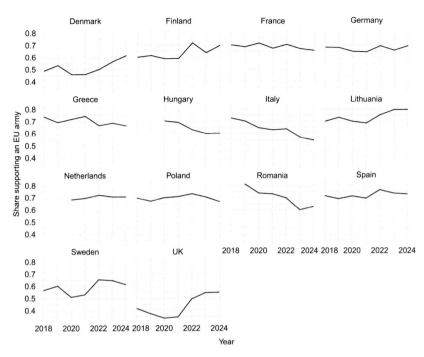

Figure 1 Support for EU army across time and EU countries

most countries.[7] Importantly, our more detailed original panel survey allows us to show how these trends differ across policy domains. Secondly, our original panel data allows us to go more in depth in terms of the significance of these time trends. What does it mean that a higher or a lower share of respondents support an EU army? We combine this data with views on EU integration and unpack the main drivers behind these shifting dynamics.

Panel data has the unique advantage of tracking individuals over time in order to see how their attitudes shift in response to changing conditions and the continuation of the conflict. It also allows more in-depth causal exploration of the interplay between ideology, output legitimacy, and security conditions. In addition to our panel structure, our series of surveys also included several experiments, which aimed to shed further causal light on questions surrounding the support for policies and the European polity.

Preliminary analyses using part of the data have been published (Moise, Dennison, and Kriesi 2023; Truchlewski, Oana, and Moise 2023; Wang and Moise 2023) and inform our current theoretical framework and empirical

---

[7] This pattern is also confirmed in Eurobarometer data presented in Appendix Figure 7.1 showing that at the beginning of the invasion a rally-round-the-flag effect surrounding the EU did happen, rally which was eventually dampened between 2022 and 2023.

goals. Our preliminary findings suggest neither a complete endorsement nor a complete rejection of the 'bellicist' logic. Instead of focusing on the question of 'whether the war resulted in polity-building' we focus on what types of polity-building are likely, given what the demand side of politics can support. Much remains to be explored, including the temporal dynamics across the three waves.

2.4.2 Operationalization of the Polity Categories

In order to operationalize the four polity categories that form our dependent variable, we take a general measure of support for the polity and specific measures of support for the various policy domains. To measure support for the polity, we use a question that asks respondents whether EU integration should go further or whether it has gone too far.[8] This measure remains constant across policy domains.[9] Then, for each specific policy domain, we use questions asking whether in that specific policy area, the respondent would like to see more centralization at the EU level or not. While there might be multiple ways of policy-specific integration (e.g., integration in the energy field need not be done via the sharing of costs, but via other means), we use these indicators as they all represent salient policy proposals discussed at the EU level at the time of data collection.

- Refugee policy: 'Each EU country should be required to accommodate a share of refugees'. – 11-point scale Agree-Disagree;
- Energy policy: 'Some experts say that moving away from Russian gas is expected to affect some EU countries more than others in the short term. Which of the following statements comes closest to your view'. Answer categories:
  - The cost of moving away from Russian gas should be a matter for each government individually;

---

[8] 'Some say European integration should be pushed forward. Others say it has already gone too far. How do you feel about this? Select a value from 0 to 10, where 0 means "European integration has already gone too far" and 10 means "European integration should be pushed further"'.

[9] Other measures, such as trust in the EU, were strong contenders for capturing general EU support. However, trust is a diffuse measure that is too unspecific to the concept of loyalty towards the polity that we aim to capture. Publics have varying degrees of trust towards a variety of actors (including Russia and Ukraine) without this implying their loyalty towards them, while trust also does not imply any preference for strengthening the EU polity which the measure of support for EU integration captures directly. Nevertheless, we perform robustness checks of the analyses in the Element with trust in Appendix Section 3 with the results remaining constant both for territorial divisions between countries, as well as for the predictors of polity attitudes statically and over time.

- The cost of moving away from Russian gas should be shared between all EU member states;
- Foreign policy: 'Foreign policy decisions, such as decisions about war and peace, should be taken at the EU level, rather than at the level of the single member states'. – 11-point scale Agree-Disagree;
- Military policy: 'The EU should create its own army'. – 11-point scale Agree-Disagree.

In order to create the four groups and harmonize measurement across our policy fields, we dichotomize our 11-point scale measures. In doing so we opt for a conservative measurement of support for policy and polity, assigning the mid-point of the scales (5) to the lack of support categories. We, thus, consider only values above 6 to indicate support for the specific policy, or for the polity in our integration question. For energy policy we code the second answer category, of sharing the cost of moving away from Russian gas, as support for centralizing the policy. In order to create the four categories we assign respondents based on whether they support the polity and the specific policy, following Table 1. Thus respondents who support both are coded as favouring a *centralized* polity, neither as *decentralized* polity, favouring policy but not polity centralization as *pooled*, and favouring polity but not policy as *reinsurance.*

In addition to our cross-sectional analyses, we also investigate the drivers of over-time change between polity types. In each section, we discuss the dynamics of change between our waves. In so doing, we discuss the vertical (e.g., from *centralized to reinsurance*) and horizontal (e.g., from *centralized to pooled*) movements in figure 1 (and subsequent descriptive figures such as Figure 3), but not diagonal (e.g., from *centralized to decentralized*) changes. We do this in order to make the changes comparable. Vertical and horizontal change requires a respondent to change only one variable, whereas diagonal change requires them to change both. This means that for practical purposes a diagonal change is less likely, as we observe (see e.g., Figure 7). We discuss these changes in detail in each section.

More generally, our dichotomization could raise several concerns regarding respondents generally placing themselves in the middle of the scale, a high correlation of polity-policy attitudes, the robustness of the effects of independent variables on the disaggregated dependent variable, or losses of information in the analysis of change. We discuss these concerns more in depth in the Appendix (Sections 1, 4, and 5) to the Element where we show that the extremes of our scales represent sizable categories, that the correlation of policy–polity attitudes is smaller than expected, that the effects of our predictors are rather stable and in the expected direction on each of the two constituent variables, and also show more detailed results in the analysis of change.

2.4.3 The Determinants of Support and Modelling Strategy

Following our theoretical framework, we focus on three types of independent variables that may affect support for the different forms of the EU polity: satisfaction with performance at the EU and the national level, ideology, trust in Ukraine, and security factors such as threat perception and economic vulnerability. In the Appendix (Section 1) to the Element we present descriptive figures for these independent variables and their variation across countries and change over time.

We perform two types of analysis across the policy fields of interest to this Element: refugee, energy, foreign policy, and military policy. The first analysis is a static analysis of our second wave (8 to 28 July 2022), where we have the larger country sample, including Portugal and Finland. Due to the categorical nature of our dependent variable, we perform a multinomial analysis. We present the results in predicted probability plots for ease of interpretation. In addition, we also present an analysis of change between waves. We first present descriptives for how the relative proportions of each group in our dependent variable change between waves 1 and 2, and then 2 and 3. Given the large number of combinations of types of change (sixteen possible changes for each wave pairing), we limit our analysis to analyzing the change in the 'centralized' group, which we argue is crucial to understanding whether we can expect policy-specific polity formation.[10] We utilize multinomial models with country-fixed effects and include both level and change for our predictors. In interpreting results we focus only on the effect of changes in our predictors on whether individuals remain in the 'centralized' category or switch to one of the other three.

For both types of models, beyond our main explanatory variables included in the coefficient plots, we also control for trust in the government, interest in politics, and include country-fixed effects. Our analysis of change suffers from possible problems related to attrition in our sample. We conduct all change analyses on the same set of respondents, who were retained in the survey across all three waves and make up about 50 per cent of the original sample. Attrition analysis reveals that our sample remains mostly balanced, despite the attrition. Respondents who are retained differ in only two factors across our dependent and independent variables. Respondents who are interested in politics are about

---

[10] In Section 5 of the Appendix, we show that the results for the other categories are symmetric.

10 per cent more likely to remain in the sample. Respondents who are in favour of an EU army are about 4 per cent more likely to remain in the sample. These modest effects, coupled with the fact that no other factors are significant, give us confidence that attrition does not present substantial bias in our analysis. The static analysis in wave 2 utilizes fully representative samples, which include the retained respondents from wave 1 together with new respondents until our original quotas were filled.

3 Refugee Policy

Between 2015 and 2022, refugee crises repeatedly tested the EU's politics, albeit in different manners. The 2015–16 crisis unleashed political conflicts between frontline and destination states (e.g., Greece vs. Germany), undermined the EU's capacity to act and find solutions (e.g., the failure of the quota system), and induced an anti-immigration backlash in public opinion. By contrast, the 2022 refugee crisis forced the EU to innovate to accommodate Ukrainian refugees by activating the Temporary Protection Directive (TPD). All in all, two different political dynamics unfolded as the two refugee crises played out in 2015 and 2022 (Moise, Dennison, and Kriesi 2023; Kriesi et al. 2024): while the far-right used the 2015 refugee crisis to garner votes, in 2022 it was less vocal. Likewise, elites and publics alike were less polarized and more welcoming of refugees in 2022 than in 2015. Finally, the refugee aspect of the Russian invasion of Ukraine was one of the most salient at the beginning of the invasion, when compared to other policy areas such as energy or defence (Moise, Dennison, and Kriesi 2023; Moise et al. 2024). In this section, we examine the nature, drivers, and temporal evolution of support for our four polity types in the refugee domain. In terms of structure, we start by descriptively mapping public preferences onto the four polity types identified in Section 2 (see Table 1): the centralized polity, the pooled polity, the reinsurance polity, and the decentralized polity. We then examine static territorial and (post-)functional divisions in these preferences before examining how changes in political attitudes over time are related to polity types.

Before proceeding to the analyses, we put forward several expectations based on existing research. First, we expect public opinion to be more in favour of a centralized or a pooled polity when it comes to the refugee policy domain, compared to other domains (Moise et al. 2024). Granting Ukrainian refugees temporary protection, including free movement, right to work and social benefits, was one of the first actions of the EU in response to Russia's invasion. The consensual policymaking with respect to refugees contrasts with the intense disagreements over, for example, sending weapons to Ukraine (which we

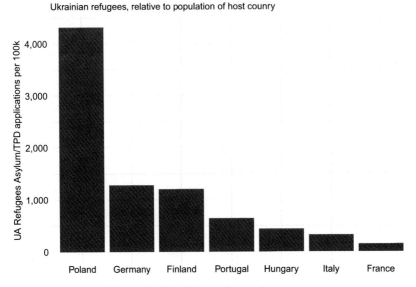

Figure 2 Ukrainian refugees by country

consider in Section 6) or enacting sanctions on Russia (which we consider in Section 4), both within and between countries.

Second, in terms of country differences, we expect that respondents in the main destination states, Poland, Germany, and Finland, should be most in favour of a centralized polity in this domain. Respondents in countries that are further away from the frontline or that do not have large numbers of refugees, such as Portugal and France, should be least in favour. Finally, respondents in countries that are frontline but not large destination states, such as Hungary, should fall somewhere in between. Figure 2 shows the number of asylum or TPD applications per country relative to the population of each country. Poland stands out as having the highest relative burden, i.e., more than 4,000 applications per 100,000.[11]

Third, concerning individual-level drivers, we expect to see fewer divisions among social groups than in other policy fields given the consensual style of policymaking and the scarce opposition by parties to the TPD. For the same reasons, we expect to see smaller effects of threat or economic vulnerability. Instead, following the existing literature (Moise, Dennison, and Kriesi 2023), we expect existing immigration attitudes to be a strong predictor in this policy field. For our temporal analysis, we expect support for the centralized and pooled polity types to be more resilient in the refugee field, compared to other policies.

---

[11] UNHCR data from 2022 until 2024, https://data.unhcr.org/en/situations/ukraine/location/680.

The findings of this section can be summarized as follows. We find the highest support for a centralized polity in refugee policy, compared to other domains. Furthermore, even those who do not support a centralized polity type still support the sharing refugees among Member States, as the pooled group is the second largest in our sample.

In terms of territorial divisions, the observed asymmetry is not as stark as in the other domains. The group preferring a centralized polity is the largest in five of the Member States included: Germany, Finland, Italy, Portugal, and Poland. France and Portugal are different: in the former, the pooled polity group is quite big and in the later preferences for centralization are followed by those for reinsurance. Hungary stands out as the only country for decentralization (and then reinsurance). The latter implies that even among the pro-Europeans there is little will to share refugees.

In functional terms, satisfaction at the EU level, support for refugee aid, and pro-immigration attitudes all have strong effects for the centralized polity. Preferences for a pooled polity remain high even among those that are not satisfied. National satisfaction is negatively related to centralization, but has a strong positive effect on support for the pooled polity type. Compared to the other policy domains we study, being satisfied with what your government did does not imply a fall-back on the national level in the refugee domain, but rather still results in a preference for pooling at the EU level. In terms of the ideational variables, again it is ideology and trust that have strong effects, but it is interesting to note that even the very far-right and those not trusting Ukraine at all still prefer the pooled polity.

In terms of over-time dynamics, we find that in general respondents shift their preferences a lot between different polity types but three patterns stand out: first, respondents use the pooled and reinsurance polity types as a safety valve to opt for coordinated European response to the refugee crisis without sacrificing sovereignty to the centralized polity. Second, over time, respondents either shift their preferences back to the centralized polity type or to the pooled one. Third and finally, it is neither threat nor vulnerability that decides whether respondents stay within or switch between polity types. Rather, the results suggest that performance evaluations at the European and national levels are strong drivers of these shifts. This indicates that neither the 'Tillian' security logic nor the 'Milwardian' social security logic has a dynamic impact on polity preferences, but it is rather internal factors that drive these shifts.

3.1 Descriptives: General Preferences for Polity Types

Figure 3 shows an overwhelming support for pooling and sharing resources in the refugee domain. The top plot shows that close to 40 per cent of respondents

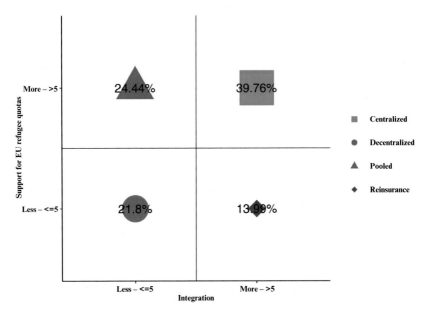

Figure 3 Polity versus policy attitudes on refugee policy

would prefer a centralized polity. The size of this group is slightly larger than in the energy and foreign policy domains, and considerably larger than that in the defence domain. What sets the refugee domain apart is that the second biggest group in our data is formed by those wanting a pooled polity who want to share the hosting of asylum-seekers in spite of not having a high loyalty to the polity (24.44 per cent). While in the other policy domains the two groups on the off-diagonal with consistent polity–policy attitudes (centralized and decentralized polity) were the larger categories, the high support for Ukrainian refugees in the current crisis makes preferences for pooling trump considerations of loyalty with most respondents located in the upper cells of Figure 3.

3.2 Territorial: Preferences for Polity Types by Country

When looking at preferences for polity types across the countries in our sample in Figure 4, we can see some notable divisions. To begin with, the group preferring a centralized polity is the largest in five out of the seven member states we consider: Germany, Finland, Italy, Portugal, and Poland. In most of these countries this group is followed by the pooled polity group, with the exception of Portugal in which the reinsurance group is the second biggest. France also closely follows the pattern of these five countries, with the centralized polity and the pooled polity groups being the largest two. Hungary stands out as the only member state among the ones analysed in which respondents preferring

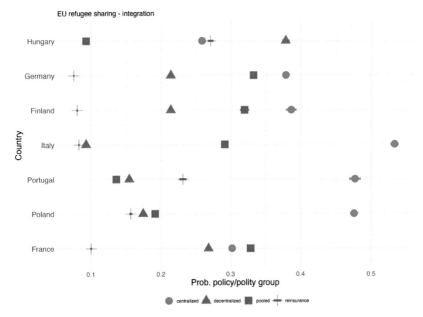

Figure 4 Preferences for polity types by country

a decentralized polity constitutes the largest group. This group is followed by the group wanting a reinsurance polity and the group wanting a centralized polity. Strikingly, the group preferring a pooled polity obtains virtually no support in Hungary suggesting that among those respondents who are not loyal to the EU polity very few would prefer to pool resources and share the hosting of refugees.

Thus, our expectations are only partly borne out. We indeed see high support for pooling in destination states: Poland, Germany, and Finland. However, we also note surprisingly high support in Portugal and Italy and remarkably low support in Hungary, despite it being a frontline state which saw a large influx of refugees in the beginning of the war. What might explain Hungarian preferences is the relatively low final number of refugees that stayed, and the anti-EU and anti-Ukraine stances of Hungary's ruling party (Madlovics and Magyar 2023).

3.3 Functional: The Effect of Individual Attitudes on Polity Types

Figure 5 shows the effects of satisfaction with refugee aid to Ukraine, support for such aid, and general immigration attitudes on support for polity types in the refugee domain. As expected, all these variables have a similar direction of effects. All three attitudes are strongly positively related to support for a

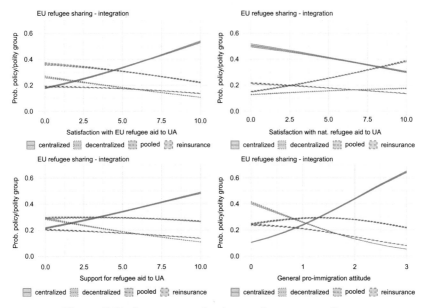

Figure 5 Performance evaluations and support – refugees

centralized polity, with effect sizes varying between a 50 percentage points increase in the probability of support in the case of pro-immigration attitudes, to a 28 percentage points increase in the case of the refugee aid variable (when moving from end-to-end of the scale in each independent variable). They are also negatively related to support for a decentralized polity but with smaller effect sizes. The only difference is that while satisfaction with the EU's performance is also negatively related to support for a pooled polity, the support for aid in general and the general pro-immigration attitudes have little to no effects on the probability to support this polity type. This is unsurprising given the large support for pooling observed in our sample.

Generally, we note that satisfaction with the way the national government handled refugee aid to Ukraine has quite different effects from these three variables. It is positively related to support for a pooled polity and negatively related to support for a centralized polity. This is important and in stark difference to our other three policy domains as we shall see in the following empirical sections. National satisfaction in the foreign policy, energy, and military domains was mostly negatively related to support for a centralized polity, an effect that we also observe here. However, in other policy domains national satisfaction increased preferences for a decentralized polity, while here it mainly increases the probability of supporting a pooled polity. In other words, in contrast to the other policy domains, satisfaction with national refugee policy does not imply opposition to organizing such a policy at the EU level.

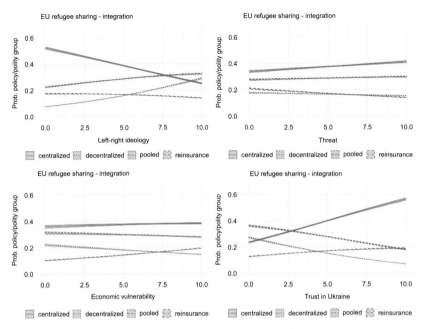

Figure 6 Ideology, threat, trust – refugees

In Figure 6, we move onto the effects of ideational and security factors (ideology, threat, trust, and economic vulnerability). In what regards ideology, the more to the right a respondent is the less likely they want a centralized polity and the more likely they want a decentralized one. Different to the other polity domains, we can see here that there is a small but significant effect on preferences for a pooled polity, preferences which nevertheless remain high along the whole ideological scale, and higher than preferences for a decentralized polity. In other words, even those on the very right would rather want a pooled polity, but followed closely by the decentralized group. Overall, when compared to other policy areas, we conclude that ideology has a weaker effect for refugee policy most likely due to the fact that attitudes on immigration (one of the other predictors in the model) are strongly correlated to ideological self-placement. Trust in Ukraine has the opposite effect to left-right ideology: it is positively related to preferences for a centralized polity and negatively related to preferences for a decentralized or a pooled one. Finally, threat and economic vulnerability have null to small effects net of the ideational and output legitimacy factors included in the model.[12]

---

[12] In Section 6 of the Appendix we also show that these results are robust to the exclusion of satisfaction with the EU's refugee policy for all policy domains.

3.4 Dynamics over Time

We now move on to the dynamic aspect of our panel data, namely observing how respondents change preferences between waves of our survey. Tables 2 and 3 present the raw data. The four columns in each table show the percentage of the members of each respective polity type that either maintain their preference (the diagonal, in bold) or change to other polity types. The final column shows the number of individuals initially in each group in wave 2. Several important patterns emerge. Between waves 1 and 2, similar to the other policy fields, the centralized and decentralized categories are the most stable, followed by the pooled category which is also much more stable in the refugee field compared to the other fields studied. Looking at changes between waves 2 and 3, the pooled category remains even more stable than the decentralized category. Between waves 1 and 2, 68 per cent of respondents stay in the centralized category, while between waves 2 and 3 this proportion increased to 77 per cent. By contrast, the share of respondents staying in the decentralized category decreases from 69 to 58 per cent, whereas in the pooled category it increases from 54 to 59 per cent. The reinsurance type of polity has 33–34 per cent of respondents staying between waves while the pooled polity has slightly below 60 per cent.

Next, the dynamics of these changes are important. We note that we see both horizontal and vertical changes in our original two-by-two. That is to say that we observe movement on both the polity and the policy dimensions of our typology. There are important flows going from the centralized polity type to

Table 2 Changes in polity groups from waves 1 to 2 – refugees

Initial cat.	Centralized	Decentralized	Pooled	Reinsurance	N
1 Centralized	**68%**	5%	16%	11%	1,988
2 Decentralized	4%	**68%**	21%	7%	635
3 Pooled	18%	23%	**54%**	6%	922
4 Reinsurance	26%	26%	13%	**34%**	526

Table 3 Changes in polity groups from waves 2 to 3 – refugees

Initial cat.	Centralized	Decentralized	Pooled	Reinsurance	N
1 Centralized	**77%**	3%	13%	7%	1,646
2 Decentralized	6%	**58%**	25%	11%	864
3 Pooled	20%	16%	**59%**	4%	1,022
4 Reinsurance	39%	15%	13%	**33%**	492

and from both the pooled and reinsurance types, of roughly equal size. In other words, those who favour a centralized polity change both in their polity attitudes (switching in and out of pooled) and their policy attitudes (switching in and out of reinsurance). This is surprising, given how deeply entrenched we usually consider attitudes towards the EU polity to be. Crisis times put these attitudes in flux, allowing greater shifts in opinion, and it is the case here in the aftermath of the Russian invasion of Ukraine. We likewise note both types of shifts in and out of the decentralized group. Between the first two waves, the decentralized group gains in size from both the pooled category and the reinsurance category. By contrast, it loses support mainly to the pooled one. This implies that the dynamics of changing support differ for those who are loyal to the EU polity and those who are not. For the latter group, sharing resources may be a more fruitful first step of persuasion.

Finally, Figure 7 shows the dynamics of change in the form of a Sankey plot. Each column corresponds to each wave in our survey. The nodes represent the

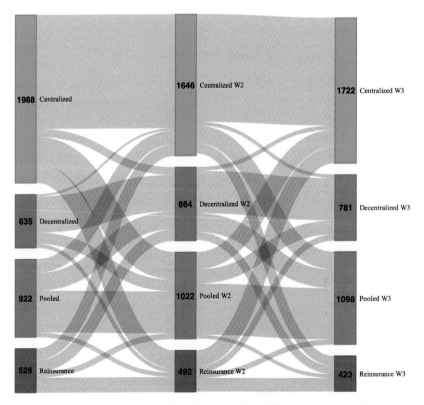

Figure 7 Refugee policy change and stability across waves[a]

[a] The number indicates the raw group size in that particular wave.

four groups, while the flows between them show where each group switches to and from. The figure suggests two additional patterns: a fading of the rally-round-the-flag effect and a bounce-back effect. On one hand, the literature would in general suggest that the initial measurement that we have in our panel is biased because it would already take into account the initial rally-round-the-flag: of course, respondents would want a more centralized polity in the aftermath of the Russian invasion of Ukraine. But what matters is whether this effect persists with other findings suggesting a fading over time (Truchlewski, Oana, and Moise 2023). The switches from waves 1 to 2 confirm such a fading effect. However, the pattern of change from waves 2 to 3 also suggests a bounce-back effect, with the polity categories gaining the most being the pooled and the centralized ones. There is thus evidence that over-time respondents consider that the European polity has to step in to solve a common problem, but this is not necessarily done at the cost of national sovereignty through centralization at the supranational level: the pooled polity works as a safety valve where anti-Europeans might take refuge and still preserve a modicum of sovereignty.

Beyond the descriptive analysis of change, we also ask what are the factors that determine such change with a particular focus on output legitimacy and security factors (ideational and other factors are controlled for and their effects can be explored in the Appendix, Section 2). For reasons of simplicity, we focus on the centralized group and ask which factors explain whether respondents remain in the centralized group or switch to other categories. While the full models, available in the Appendix, include both levels and changes in predictors, for ease of interpretation we focus here only on change. Thus, the predicted probabilities in Figure 8 can be interpreted as the probability to remain in the centralized group or switch to other groups, for varying levels of change in the predictors.

While the security literature suggests that external threats and economic vulnerability should lead to increasing preferences for polity centralization, Figure 8 finds little evidence for such effects in the refugee policy field net of ideational and output legitimacy factors. What we find is evidence for endogenous polity formation: the more satisfied with the EU refugee policy respondents are, the more prone they are to stick to the centralized polity and the less likely they are to opt for other types of polities. The same applies to the national polity: if respondents are satisfied with their national governments' refugee policy, they are still counter-intuitively prone to support a centralized European polity. This stands in stark contrast to the effects we observe for other policy fields where satisfaction with the national policy leads to a lower likelihood of staying in the centralized category. This difference in policy domains can be reflective of

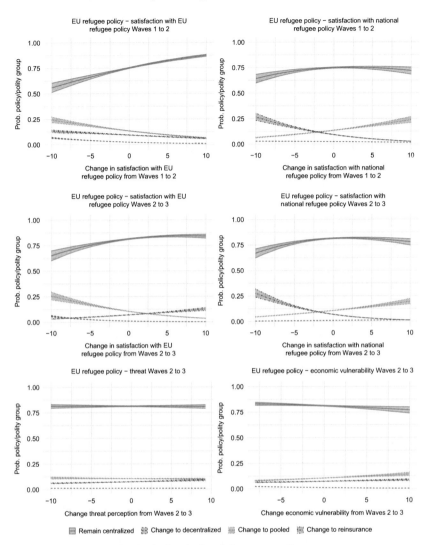

Figure 8 Analysis of change – refugees

a common underlying positive attitude towards immigration (on top of the one captured by the variable on immigration attitudes).

3.5 Conclusion

Our evidence suggests that refugee policy has the highest share of individuals preferring a *centralized* polity, followed by a *pooled polity* (further integration in refugee policy without broader political integration). This stands in stark contrast with other policy fields which show a greater degree of dissensus. Also in contrast with other policy fields, we see fewer territorial divisions, as only

Hungary does not have a plurality of respondents that are in favour of a *centralized* polity. Our analysis of the individual drivers of support shows that a higher satisfaction with the EU's handling of refugees is strongly related to preferring a *centralized polity*, while satisfaction with national refugee policy increases the probability of being in the *pooled* category, as opposed to the *decentralized* one as observed in other policy fields. Overall, satisfaction and ideological variables have a strong impact in support for polity types, while security concerns, including threat and economic vulnerability, play a much more limited role.

4 Energy Policy

Because of very asymmetric national energy profiles and the cost of adapting those due to high investment costs, we expect to see high levels of divisions between and within EU member states in terms of preferences for pooling energy resources in Figure 10. These divergences are compounded by the varying energy dependence on Russia and the geography of certain countries being landlocked and pipelocked: Slovakia and Hungary, for instance, do not have the ability to quickly import liquefied natural gas through port terminals, as Germany did after February 2022. To cap it all, energy profiles and energy dependence are exacerbated at the individual level due to socioeconomic vulnerabilities (Natili and Visconti 2023). Thus, these asymmetric

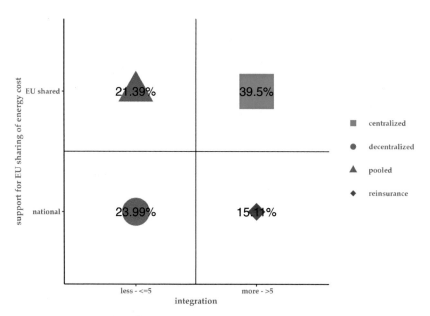

Figure 9 Polity versus policy attitudes on energy policy

problem pressures can open territorial and functional conflicts (Caramani 2015) that create incoherent or polarized coalitions for polity formation in the energy policy field.

The findings of this section can be summarized as follows. First, descriptive evidence suggests very high support for the pooled and centralized polity types. Nevertheless, there is a large minority wanting a decentralized polity, a group that is slightly larger than those wanting a pooled polity (in contrast to the relative size of these groups in the refugee policy domain). Consequently, among those respondents with low loyalty to the polity, there is a high preference for resorting to the national level.

Second, concerning the territorial dimension of preferences, the asymmetry of the crisis resulted in strong divides among respondents in three groups of countries: respondents in Italy, Portugal, and Poland have strong preferences for a centralized polity; in Hungary, Germany, and France are heavily divided between centralizing and decentralizing; respondents in Finland stand out as having the highest preferences for a decentralized polity, followed by a reinsurance one (somewhat counter-intuitively given its geographic location).

Third, concerning the individual drivers of support, we find that satisfaction at the EU level and support for sanctions have the potential to mitigate polity support and/or skepticism, as they are positively related to support for a centralized polity and negatively related to support for a decentralized polity. There is, however, an inverse relation (with smaller effect sizes) in terms of national satisfaction. Beyond performance evaluations, ideology and trust in Ukraine also have a substantive impact on preferences for polity formation, contrary to threat and economic vulnerability for which we find small to null effects.

Fourth, when inquiring into over-time dynamics, the centralized and decentralized polity types are the most stable, while the pooled and reinsurance ones experience important fluctuations between waves of our panel. Usually, respondents who preferred the pooled polity type switch primarily to the decentralized type, while those who preferred the reinsurance type move to the centralized one. Satisfaction with EU and national sanctions are again the most important predictors of staying in the centralized polity.

4.1 Descriptives: General Preferences for Polity Types

Descriptively, in terms of the share of the four groups among our sample, we notice in Figure 9 that a plurality of the respondents prefers a centralized polity (39.5 per cent), and more so than in foreign and military policies, and only slightly less than in refugee policy. Likewise, 21.4 per cent of respondents opt for a pooled polity. In other words, almost 61 per cent of respondents voice a strong preference for one form or another of pooling and/or sharing of resources and decisions. These possible coalitions between respondents who prefer a centralized polity and pooled polity is the second biggest in the realm of energy policy (after refugee policy at 64.2 per cent, with foreign policy at 58 per cent and defence policy at 51.8 per cent following).

By contrast, there are only 15.1 per cent of respondents who opt for the reinsurance polity in energy policy. Given that this type of respondent is loyal to the EU polity but wants resources and decisions to remain at the national level in this policy domain, they could be easily swayed to move into a pooled or a centralized polity, should the need arise (e.g., crises intensity increasing). If we factor in preferences for the reinsurance polity, the coalition that could support some form of further polity building in the realm of energy policy broadens to 76 per cent of respondents. Taking all the three polity preferences together, it seems that the postfunctional consensus for polity formation is pretty large and it mostly depends on how policymakers will balance the preferences of voters who prefer a pooled or a reinsurance polity.

Such a possible coalition between respondents of the centralized, pooled and reinsurance polities nonetheless faces a powerful minority expressing support for the decentralized polity: almost 24 per cent of respondents. This powerful minority is however not as consequential as in other policy domains: while it is bigger than in refugee policy domain (21.8 per cent), it is smaller than in the domain of foreign policy (26.4 per cent) and defence policy (27.6 per cent).

4.2 Territorial: Preferences for Polity Types by Country

The energy policy domain is marked by high heterogeneity between the countries in our sample given different levels of energy dependence on Russia. Figure 10 offers a visualization of this heterogeneity. The left-hand graph plots total gas imports from Russia (as share of all gas imports) against the burden of public debt (as a share of GDP). It shows how countries are dependent on Russia for their gas, and how fragile they are in terms of public capacity to fund alternatives and, perhaps most importantly, to cushion the blow of any sanctions via fiscal transfers for their electorates.

In this two-dimensional space, we can group countries into four categories and we predict that these four categories should on average have different preferences for the EU polity in the realm of energy policy. The first group encompasses countries that are dependent on Russia for gas, but robust economically (bottom right corner: this group includes Germany, Poland, and Finland[13] in

---

[13] Finland, like France, is special also because it has quite a particular energy mix with high nuclear energy capacity.

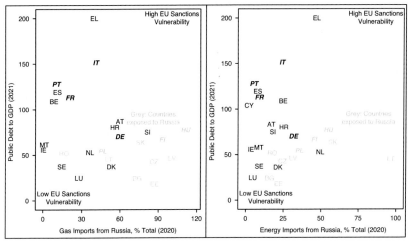

Figure 10 Public debt to GDP and Russian energy dependence across the EU

Data source: Data on energy are taken from Eurostat, which calculates the volume of energy imports compared to the volume of energy consumption. Note that some countries import more gas than they need because they re-export it. Data on public debt are taken from the World Economic Outlook of the International Monetary Fund (Version of October 2022). In the figures, 'countries exposed to Russia' means either bordering Russia or having in the recent past experienced conflicts with Russia (e.g., former communist countries).

our sample but also other countries such as Luxembourg, Netherlands, or Denmark). These countries should prefer, on average, a pooled polity that helps to withstand the cost of sanctions but does not centralize policymaking to such an extent that it curtails sovereignty and imposes costs on economically robust countries.

The second group comprises countries that are dependent on Russia for gas, and weak economically (top right corner: this group includes Hungary and Italy in our sample, but also others such as Greece, Austria, and Croatia). These countries should prefer a centralized polity that would help with solidaristic safety nets and socialize solidarity in order to spread the cost of sanctions.

The third group consists of countries that are not dependent on gas for Russia and economically vulnerable and thus could fall pray to a spillover of costs from energy markets to other markets or to inflation – and which could as a result back opposition to energy sanctions and/or more polity building in the field of energy (top left corner: Portugal and France, in our sample). These countries should, on average, display stronger profiles for the reinsurance polity, that is, a polity that intervenes in a decentralized manner only if the unforeseen need arises to deal with a vulnerability.

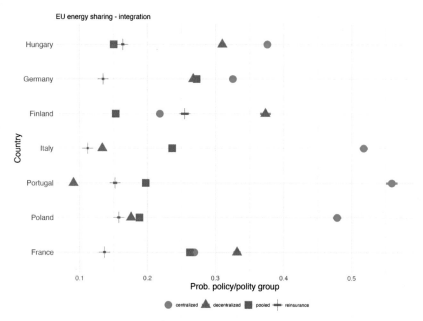

Figure 11 Preferences for polity types by country

The fourth group includes countries that are neither dependent on Russia for gas nor vulnerable economically in terms of budgetary power (Malta, Ireland, and Romania). These countries should have a strong preference for a decentralized polity. However, none of these countries fall within our sample.

In terms of territorial divides, Figure 11 shows a fair amount of country heterogeneity and our hypotheses are only partially confirmed. Respondents in Italy, Portugal, and Poland all prefer a centralized polity to the other types, with the pooled polity category coming in as a far second. Hungary, Germany, and France stand out as the most divided countries. In these three countries preferences for a centralized polity and for a decentralized polity have similar values indicating a bigger societal divide in the kind of polity respondents want. Nevertheless, while in Hungary this societal divide really is just split between centralized-decentralized, in France and Germany, the pooled polity type also enters the mix indicating that in these countries, those that are not loyal to the polity are heavily split in their pooling preferences. Finally, in what regards energy sharing, Finland is the country that stands out as the only one in which respondents are more strongly in favour of a decentralized polity compared to all other polity types. Preferences for a decentralized polity are followed by preferences for a reinsurance one, indicating that respondents in Finland are heavily against the pooling of resources in the energy policy domain. This is quite surprising given the high reliance of Finland on Russian energy and the heavy consequences of sanctions on rethinking energy sources and mitigating price rises.

4.3 Functional: The Effect of Individual Attitudes on Polity Types

We now move on from territorial divisions to functional divisions. We start with the output legitimacy. Figure 12 suggests higher satisfaction with EU sanctions increases preferences for a centralized polity at the expense of the decentralized polity (with an effect size of more than 20 percentage points if one were to move on the opposite sides of the satisfaction scale) and the less one wants a decentralized polity (with an effect size of almost 25 percentage points). Thus, EU measures have the potential to mitigate polity skepticism and consequently polity preferences are at least partially endogenous to European crisis responses. Satisfaction with the EU measures also slightly increases the probability of being in the reinsurance group and slightly decreases the probability of being in the pooled polity group, suggesting that satisfaction might be coupled more with loyalty towards the polity, than preferences for pooling means and decisions.

When it comes to satisfaction with the actions of the Member States' governments, we observe an inverse relationship between this and preferences for a centralized polity. Granted, if one is already satisfied with what the actions

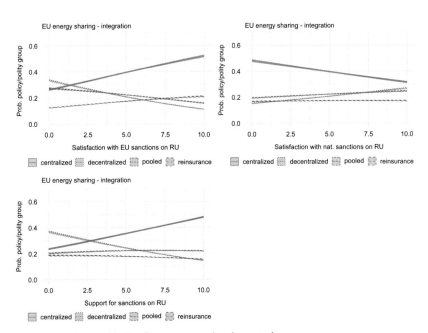

Figure 12 Performance evaluations and support – energy

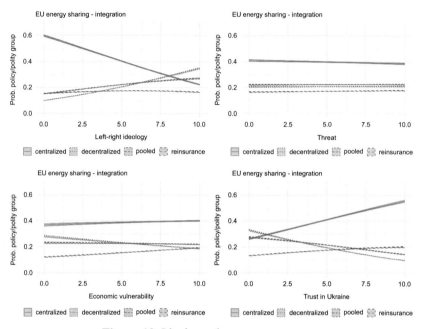

Figure 13 Ideology, threat, trust – energy

of the strong sub-units of the polity, the incentive to centralize is lower. In line with this, there is also a positive effect of national satisfaction on decentralizing (albeit smaller than the one on centralizing), while there are little to no effects on the mixed polity types – pooled and reinsurance. Finally, in terms of support for sanctioning Russia, irrespective of the level at which it is implemented, we observe results similar to those obtained for the satisfaction with the EU measures.

In Figure 13 we turn to ideational and security factors. The results show a strong effect of ideology and trust in Ukraine on polity preferences, while it suggests that security factors – economic vulnerability and threat perceptions stemming from the invasion – play a much smaller role even in the energy domain, a domain with strong asymmetric implications in what regards the economic outcomes of the policies taken. The top left plot shows the strong effect of ideology: the more a respondent self-places themselves to the right, the more they support a decentralized policy when it comes to sharing energy costs (25 percentage point increase along the 0–10 ideology scale) and the less they want a centralized policy (38 percentage point decrease along the 0–10 ideology scale). Along similar lines, the bottom right plot shows strong effects of trust in Ukraine: the more one trusts Ukraine, the more one prefers a centralized polity and the less one prefers a decentralized one. Furthermore, trust in Ukraine is also positively associated with preferences for a reinsurance polity and negatively associated with preferences for a pooled polity, suggesting a strong association with the polity loyalty of respondents in particular. By contrast, threat perceptions and economic vulnerability have no to small effects net of the other factors included in the model.

4.4 Dynamics over Time

We now move on to the analysis of change asking which polity category is most preferred and most stable over time, and if respondents change preferences, which polity category do they switch to? Our empirics suggest that the centralized and decentralized categories are the biggest and the most stable, while respondents tend to move in and out of the pooled and reinsurance polities to the other two categories. Most importantly, our empirics confirm to a certain extent the coalitional politics between groups preferring pooled, reinsurance, and centralized polities are very much possible, which indicates that policy-makers have some leeway in shaping polity formation – provided they can convince their electorates.

These changes vary in our three waves. Let us have a look in turn, starting with switches from waves 1 to 2 (see Table 4). The most stable polity categories are centralized and decentralized: here, 67 and 63 per cent of respondents respectively stay in their initial categories. Most of the respondents who opted for centralized polity in wave 1 moved on to the pooled polity (15 per cent) and the reinsurance polity (12 per cent). Those who opted to move away from the decentralized polity rather moved towards the pooled polity (24 per cent) than the reinsurance polity. By contrast, very few people move between the centralized and the decentralized polity types (between 6 and 7 per cent of respondents). All in all, the change between waves 1 and 2 suggests that people either stick to their guns in terms of polity preferences or move towards more pooling in general. The change between waves 2 and 3 provides further evidence for the stability of the centralized and decentralized polity types and the flexibility offered to respondents by the pooled and reinsurance types

Table 4 Changes in polity groups from waves 1 to 2 – energy

Initial cat.	Centralized	Decentralized	Pooled	Reinsurance	N
1 Centralized	**67%**	7%	15%	12%	1,726
2 Decentralized	6%	**63%**	24%	7%	657
3 Pooled	18%	27%	**48%**	8%	711
4 Reinsurance	36%	21%	13%	**30%**	592

Table 5 Changes in polity groups from waves 2 to 3 – energy

Initial cat.	Centralized	Decentralized	Pooled	Reinsurance	N
1 Centralized	**73%**	4%	11%	12%	1,546
2 Decentralized	8%	**62%**	22%	8%	837
3 Pooled	21%	23%	**49%**	6%	811
4 Reinsurance	40%	13%	14%	**33%**	460

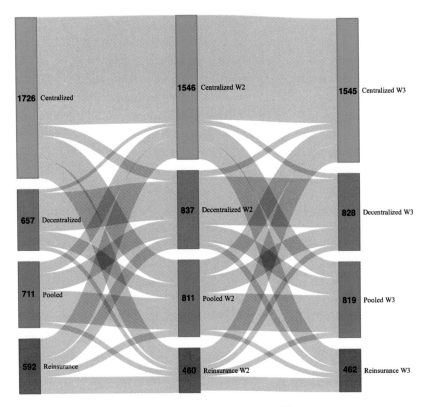

Figure 14 Energy policy change and stability across waves

(see Table 5). There is still very little movement between centralized and decentralized polity types, while the pooled and reinsurance types of polities function as a flexibility valve for respondents who change their minds on what polity type is best in their opinion in terms of energy policy.

Figure 14 shows that the largest change occurs between waves 1 and 2, as the centralized and reinsurance groups shrink and the pooled and decentralized grow. While there are also intense flows between waves 2 and 3, the relative sizes of groups do not change. What is visible, through the thickness of the flows, is the relative stability of the centralized and decentralized groups,

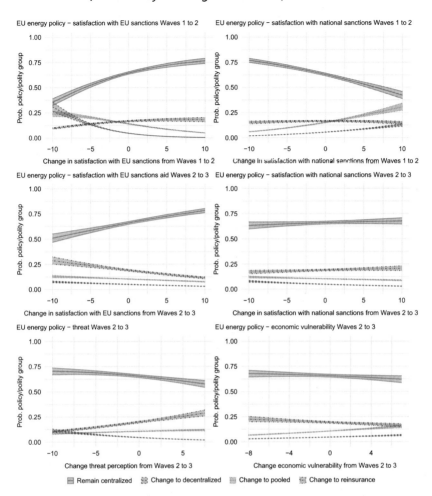

Figure 15 Analysis of change – energy

compared to pooled and reinsurance. The majority of respondents in the former two groups retain their status, while for the latter a majority switch in and out. It is also noteworthy who switches in and out of the pooled and reinsurance groups. The centralized group contributes to both, but receives more support from the reinsurance group, suggesting that it is easier to persuade to pool resources and/or decisions those who already have loyalty towards the polity. Conversely, the decentralized group both loses and gains individuals from the pooled category, suggesting that policy attitudes are more malleable than polity ones.

What determines then the change of polity preferences? In Figure 15, we focus on the effect of performance evaluations and security factors asking whether a change in polity preferences is endogenous to the evaluation of responses to a crisis (satisfaction) or whether it is driven by interactions with external factors (threat and economic vulnerability).[14] The results suggest that change between polity types is mostly driven by satisfaction, and to a much lower extent by the materiality of the crisis in energy policy itself. The higher the change in satisfaction with EU sanctions between waves 1 and 2 of our survey, the higher the probability of remaining centralized and slightly higher probability of switching to reinsurance, and almost zero probability of switching from centralized to decentralized. To a certain extent this pattern remains when we analyse the change from waves 2 to 3, with the only change being that more satisfied respondents now are less likely to switch to a reinsurance polity type. Likewise, satisfaction with national sanctions presents a mirror image: the more respondents become satisfied between waves 1 and 2 with national sanctions, to less likely they are to remain in the centralized polity and the more likely they are to switch to the pooled polity (although this pattern disappears in the change from waves 2 to 3).

The magnitude of the effects for threat perception and economic vulnerability are smaller, but their effects are still substantively worth noting. Increasing threat perceptions have a flat effect on remaining in the centralized polity but a positive impact on the probability of switching to a reinsurance polity. This makes sense, since greater threats increase the need for strengthening already existing national capacity, rather than transferring such capacity (and creating it ex nihilo) to the EU level. Interestingly, increased threat perception reduces the probability of switching from centralized to decentralized to almost zero. Respondents hence seem to prefer some form of engagement of the EU level under threat to having national-level policymaking only. Finally, while the effect of change in economic vulnerability is small, the pattern of remaining in the centralized polity and switching to other types of polities changes. Respondents who are more vulnerable economically are as likely to stay in the centralized polity but are also more likely to choose the pooled polity.

4.5 Conclusion

In the realm of energy policy, respondents clearly demand a centralized polity (with the pooled polity coming second in preferences), which is in line with other findings in the literature (Nicoli, Duin, and Burgoon 2023) and signals that a European risk-sharing logic is desired by respondents. Similar to refugee policy domain, here as well preferences for polity types are strongly associated with performance evaluations in this domain, suggesting that the way the

---

[14] Ideational and other factors are included in the model and are explored in Appendix Section 2.

European polity reacts to a crisis deeply influences polity preferences. Likewise, over-time change in polity preferences is mostly influenced by changes in such policy satisfaction. Thus, the EU's responses to crises can ease or harden the democratic postfunctional constrain on policymakers. This is surprising for energy policy, given the strong asymmetries in energy dependence and fiscal capacity to meet energy needs and compensate those affected. We note however, that there are important territorial divisions that might be hard to overcome, with respondents in Italy, Portugal and Poland being more in favour of a centralized polity, respondents in Finland being the least in favour, and Hungary, Germany, and France showing mixed preferences for polity types.

5 Foreign Policy

In this section, we look more closely at public preferences regarding the EU's foreign policy. The foreign policy of the EU is both a source of strength and weakness for the EU polity: due to the structure of its consensus-based decision-making, the EU can either manage to speak with one voice or can quickly descend into paralysis as even the smallest of its Member States can veto decisions. The latter problem can be dubbed the Polish minority problem or the 'minority of one', in the words of Rousseau: in the eighteenth-century Polish-Lithuanian parliament (*Sejm*), any member could effectively veto any bill through *liberum veto* (Wheeler 2011). One consequence of this system was that vetoes could easily be exploited by foreign powers who could manipulate members of the Sejm. As a result, American founding fathers deemed the Polish system poisonous and sought to avoid it (Levitsky and Ziblatt 2023). The EU faces a similar dilemma whereby individual governments can veto and, hence, the structure of foreign policy decision-making can be exploited both by individual member states and by geopolitical adversaries (for example, Russia may exploit Hungary's veto on sanctions and Ukraine aid).

In foreign policy, this problem is exacerbated in compound polities like the EU because each sub-unit wants to maintain autonomy and sovereignty as economies of scale are much less tangible in diplomacy than in material policies like defence or energy. Path dependence and geography can reinforce this demand for autonomy. Countries bordering a crisis-prone region may want to upload their policy solution to the whole polity, while countries far away may be reluctant to share the cost of a problem that is not theirs. For instance, Portugal and Ireland may not necessarily share Poland's and Finland's hypothetical view that defence policy should be strengthened. Conversely, countries bordering revisionist empires may not want to endorse polity-wide positions that are conciliatory rather than defence-oriented.

The findings of this section can be summarized as follows. First, the descriptive evidence points out that the lion's share of respondents (around 38 per cent) support a centralized polity in foreign policy and almost 20 per cent prefer a pooled polity. Consequently, almost 60 per cent of respondents support a more unified EU foreign policy. However, a strong minority favours a decentralized polity.

Second, regarding territorial divisions, the relative symmetry of the crisis means that respondents from several countries lean towards a centralized polity. Support for a centralized polity is highest in Portugal, Italy, Poland, Hungary, and Germany. Contrary to Macron's rhetoric of European strategic autonomy, French respondents are the most supportive of a decentralized polity. This discrepancy indicates that the hands of French policymakers are tied by a reluctant public opinion.

Third, functional variables underline that satisfaction with national and EU actions is an important driver of polity preferences, suggesting that policy responses to crises can shape preferences for the polity. Examining the role of ideology, we show that left-wing respondents prefer a centralized and reinsurance polity. Respondents who feel more threatened and more economically vulnerable in light of the invasion show greater support for a centralized polity.

Fourth and finally, our dynamic analysis reveals that, similarly to the other policy domains, the size of the polity groups is quite stable between waves 2 and 3 (we do not have measures of foreign policy support for our wave 1). Nevertheless, we can observe that while the centralized group has symmetric gains and losses in respondents from the pooled and reinsurance group, the decentralized group loses more than it gains, especially from the pooled group, resulting in a net decrease in this group. In terms of the predictors of change, again similar to the other policy domains, changes in performance evaluations are strongly associated with switching groups, whereas changes in threat perceptions and economic vulnerability have little predictive power net of these other factors.

5.1 Descriptives: General Preferences for Polity Types

We begin by analyzing how respondents from our survey cluster in the four polity types that represent our dependent variable. Figure 16 presents the size of these four groups by operationalizing loyalty towards the polity with preferences for further European integration and policy attitudes with preferences for centralization in the foreign policy domain.

The graph indicates that when it comes to the EU's foreign policy, the most preferred polity type when it comes to foreign policy is the centralized

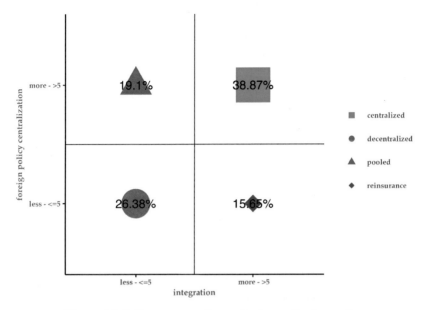

Figure 16 Polity versus policy attitudes on foreign policy

polity (policy centralization with high loyalty for the polity) with 39 per cent of respondents. The second most preferred category however is now the decentralized polity: these are respondents who neither support EU integration, nor would like foreign policy to be centralized. In the third category are those in favour of a pooled polity (centralization without strong loyalty) and the fourth and smallest category is now the reinsurance polity (coordination with strong loyalty). What is worth underlining from these descriptives is that a pro-centralization coalition between those respondents who are primarily in favour of a centralized polity and those who prefer a pooled polity represents a majority of respondents: 57.97 per cent. In Schattschneiderian terms (Hacker and Pierson 2014; Busemeyer, Abrassart, and Nezi 2021), it means that EU politicians could rest their policies on this coalition of respondents that all prefer pooling foreign policy. The calculus of the pooled polity group is more utilitarian than idealistic: therefore, as long as a centralized foreign policy delivers for national governments, these respondents are likely to remain supporters of a centralized foreign policy.

5.2 Territorial: Preferences for Polity Types by Country

It is difficult to predict the preferences of states when it comes to pooling their foreign policies. On the one hand, small countries should tend to

bandwagon and align behind more powerful states as well as exploit the power
gained by being able to co-decide the foreign policy of a bigger centralized polity. Giving up certain policy positions would then be compensated by greater
power and coercive capacities at the European level. Big states, by contrast,
should also embrace this policy because they can influence a common foreign
policy much more. Thus both big and small states should be in favour of a
centralized polity. On the other hand, however, small states may be reluctant to
pool foreign policy especially if it would be too misaligned with their own preferences – for instance, the Baltics may fear that bigger countries would prefer
to appease a revisionist power rather than confront it. Likewise, bigger countries would be wary of giving a seat at the table to small countries and allow
them to 'upload' and 'Europeanize' their foreign policy goals. More importantly, big powers looking to coordinate their foreign policy should be wary of
small states that can veto collective action.

    We therefore have no strong theoretical expectations. Figure 17 suggests
that the respondents most convinced about the centralized polity are to be
found in Italy, Portugal, and Poland. The same applies to Hungary and Germany but here respondents are very much divided between the centralized
and the decentralized polity, with the pooled polity coming a close third in
Germany. Finland is even more divided as the preferences between the two
extremes are almost equal and a sizeable share of the respondents (above 20
per cent) expresses preferences for the pooled polity. French respondents are

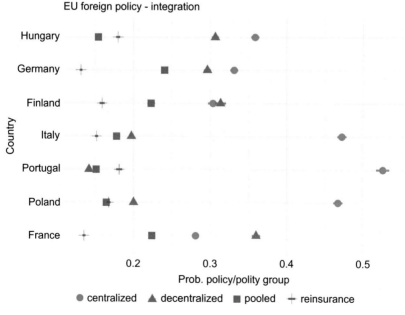

Figure 17 Preferences for polity types by country

the most idiosyncratic: their preferences for the centralized polity are the lowest (which goes against French policymakers' aim of 'strategic autonomy') and their preferences for a decentralized polity are the highest (around 35 per cent of respondents). However, the French respondents wanting to build foreign capacity in the centre of the European polity are still a majority.

5.3 Functional: The Effect of Individual Attitudes on Polity Types

The section on descriptives suggested that a majority of respondents is in favour of a centralized EU foreign policy, with their degree of loyalty for the EU polity varying. We now move on to a more inferential analysis, asking what predictors shape support for our four ideal polity types in foreign policy.

Figure 18 visualizes the effect of output legitimacy predictors and predictors related to general support for the policy (satisfaction with EU military aid to Ukraine, satisfaction with *national* military aid to Ukraine, support for military aid to Ukraine and support for increasing national military capacity). Satisfaction with EU military aid to Ukraine primarily impacts preferences for the centralized and the decentralized forms of polity: the more one is satisfied with the EU's aid to Ukraine, the more one prefers the EU to take the shape of a centralized polity. Conversely, higher satisfaction decreases preferences for a decentralized polity (the same results apply to support for military aid to Ukraine). Satisfaction with national military aid has the opposite effect: the

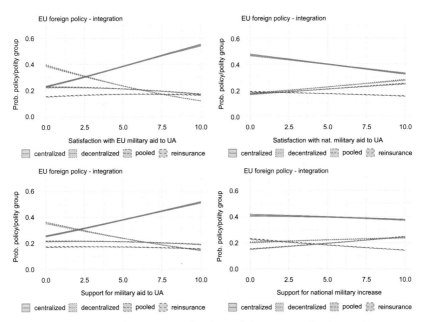

Figure 18 Performance evaluations and support – foreign policy

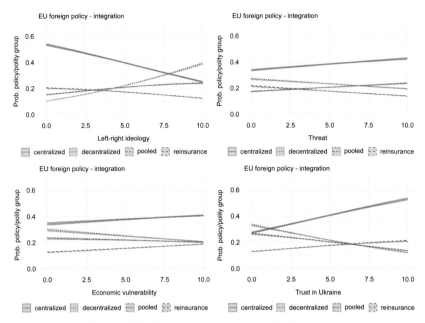

Figure 19 Ideology, threat, trust – foreign policy

more national governments are seen as well-performing units, the more there is support for a decentralized but *also for a pooled polity* and the less support there is for a centralized polity. In other words, respondents do not necessarily think in binary terms about the EU: satisfaction does not lead to a trade-off between a centralized and decentralized polity but leaves place for other types of polities to be supported (results are similar for support for increasing national military capacity).

Figure 19 vizualises the effect of ideational and security factors. Three variables go in a similar direction as far as preferences for a centralized polity in foreign policy go: the higher the perceived threat, the higher the economic vulnerability, and the higher the trust in Ukraine, the higher the preferences for a centralized polity in EU foreign policy and the lower the preferences for a decentralized polity. Threat and economic vulnerability show very small effect sizes, above and beyond trust in Ukraine and ideology. Concerning ideology, on the left respondents prefer most strongly a centralized polity and then a reinsurance polity, while right-wing respondents would rather have a decentralized polity first and a pooled polity second.

5.4 Dynamics over Time

If in the previous section we looked at the static predictors of preferences for polity types, in this section we focus on explaining the extent to which

Table 6 Changes in polity groups from waves 2 to 3 – foreign policy

Initial cat.	Centralized	Decentralized	Pooled	Reinsurance	N
1 Centralized	**72%**	4%	10%	14%	1,537
2 Decentralized	8%	**61%**	25%	7%	999
3 Pooled	25%	24%	**44%**	7%	696
4 Reinsurance	44%	13%	14%	**29%**	499

our respondents change their polity preferences over time and the predictors associated with such change.

Table 6 and Figure 20 show the extent to which individuals in each polity type switched to a different polity type from waves 2 to 3 in our survey.[15] We first note the high stability of the centralized category, with 72 per cent of respondents maintaining their preference over time. Second, we also note substantive shares of individuals in the pooled and reinsurance groups who switch to the centralized category. These two categories are also the most dynamic ones in our data (losing and/or gaining more respondents over time).

Examining Figure 20 in more in-depth we also note that the centralized type gains equal and substantive shares of respondents from both the reinsurance category and the pooled category over time, whereas the decentralized type mostly gains respondents from the pooled category. This indicates that it is mostly those respondents without loyalty to the polity to begin with that can turn against pooling resources over time. Furthermore, while the gains and losses in the centralized category are rather symmetric, making the size of this group quite stable over time, the decentralized group 'loses' more respondents than it 'gains' (especially in what regards the pooled group) resulting in net decreases of this group in wave 3.

Figure 21 shows our multinomial analysis of change. Two findings from the figure are similar to the findings in other policy domains. First, the strongest predictor for remaining in the centralized category is satisfaction with EU military aid to Ukraine. Those respondents whose satisfaction with military aid increases are more than 75 per cent likely to remain in the centralized category. Furthermore, increases in satisfaction are coupled with decreases in switching to any other category. Second, similar to the other policy domains, we can see that changes in the threat stemming from the war and economic vulnerability are poorer predictors of change in polity types, at least when taking into account

---

[15] As in the previous analyses we only examine changes from wave a 2 to 3 when it comes to foreign policy due to question availability in only these two waves.

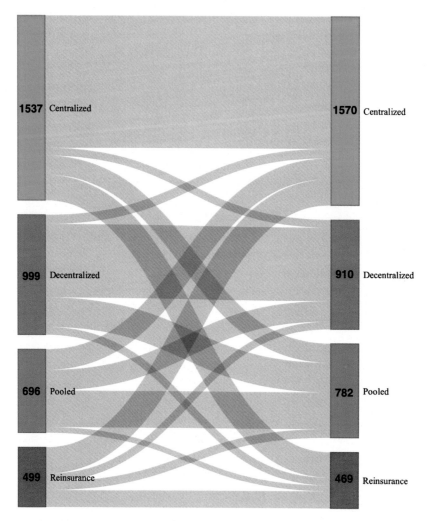

Figure 20 Foreign policy change and stability across waves 2 and 3

ideational and output legitimacy factors. This further underscores the idea that polity attitudes are heavily dependent on performance and output legitimacy, more so than on the threats stemming from the crisis. Finally, the impact of satisfaction with national policy is similar to that of its impact in waves 2 to 3 for military and energy policy, namely null. In the other policy fields, we saw that there was a negative impact of satisfaction with national policy on remaining in the centralized group, but that effect was mostly visible at the beginning of the crisis, from waves 1 to 2.

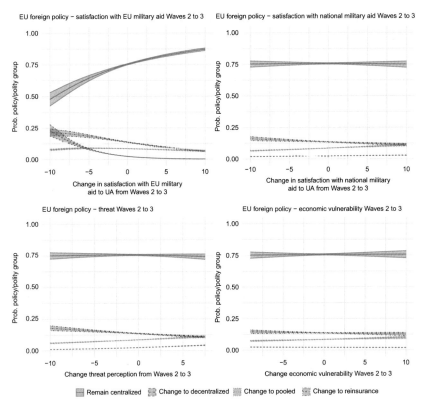

Figure 21 Analysis of change – foreign policy

5.5 Conclusion

Foreign policy falls in the middle of the policy domains we study when it comes to support for the centralized polity type, with slightly lower support than refugee and energy policy, and more support than military policy. Compared to refugee policy, foreign policy shows starker territorial divisions. The same three countries have the highest share of respondents in favour of a centralized polity: Italy, Portugal, and Poland, followed by Hungary and Germany who are also more heterogeneous. Finland and France show deeper divisions, with majorities in favour of a decentralized polity. In functional terms, we see that satisfaction with EU military policy plays a similar role to other policy fields, increasing the probability of favouring a centralized compared to a decentralized polity. National satisfaction shows the opposite, although less pronounced, trend. Interestingly, and differing from military policy, pacifism (proxied through lack of support for increasing national military capacity) does not play a role in shaping polity preferences when it comes to foreign policy. Ideology is an important driver of support with the left being more in favour of centralizing while the right is more in favour of decentralizing. Differently from energy and refugee policy, but similarly to military policy, threat and economic vulnerability have a significant, if small, effect. Higher threat and higher economic vulnerability are related to stronger support for a centralized polity. However, these results are not confirmed in our analysis of change, where changes in neither has an important impact in driving changes in support.

6 Military Policy

This section looks at polity preferences in the military domain. An EU army, perhaps the oldest of the European failed institutions, was the first truly centralized policy to be on the cards even before the Treaty of Rome in 1957. The Treaty of Paris, first discussed in 1950 and finally rejected in 1954 by the French, would have established a common European force within NATO only a few years after the most devastating conflict that the continent had ever experienced. This road not taken has been back on the agenda due to the increasingly isolationist stance of the Republican party in the United States, Trump's comments undermining NATO, and a resurgent and belligerent Russia. Studying the defence domain is particularly important for examining the bellicist logic of polity formation: the threat stemming from the Russian invasion of Ukraine should result in greater demand for centralization in this domain. Nevertheless, given the structure of the polity and the distribution of competencies in the defence domain, with strong sub-units and virtually exclusive competence at the level of the Member States, but also with security guarantees coming from the NATO umbrella, we expect to see lower support for centralization in the defence domain, especially in the short term (Moise, Truchlewski, and Oana 2024).

Our findings in this section can be summarized as follows. In terms of descriptive findings, the biggest share of respondents (around 33.2 per cent) support a centralized polity in the defence domain (which is significantly less than in all other policy domains that we investigate), and 18.6 per cent prefer a pooled polity. Almost 51.8 per cent, therefore, support a common European army in some form. Nevertheless, in line with the expectations above, defence is also the policy domain with the highest preferences for a decentralized polity (27.6 per cent).[16]

In what regards divisions at the territorial level, country preferences are divided into two groups, with one country being free-standing. On one side, Hungarian, German and Finnish respondents prefer a decentralized polity, with

---

[16] See Table 11 for a comparative summary off all the descriptive data on our four policy fields.

preferences for a centralized and reinsurance polity coming second. On the other, respondents in Italy, Portugal, and Poland clearly want a centralized polity. Given that Poland is strongly pro-NATO, this suggests that respondents do not necessarily see a trade-off between NATO and a possible EU army. Finally, French respondents give an almost equal weight to a pooled, a centralized, and a decentralized polity. Forming decisive coalitions for an EU army in France would, therefore, be difficult.[17] When it comes to individual-level predictors of support, satisfaction with and support for EU military aid to Ukraine and support for increasing national military capacity positively impact preference for a centralized polity and negatively those for a decentralized polity. Threat, economic vulnerability, and trust in Ukraine, have similar effects. In terms of ideology, (very) right-wing voters prefer a decentralized polity.

Finally, in terms of dynamics over time, not only is military policy the least supported, but support is the least stable, compared to other policy domains. Only 64 per cent of those wanting a centralized polity in wave 1 remain in this group in wave 2. At the same time, a majority of those switching from pooled and reinsurance go to the decentralized category. The result is a drastic shrinking of support for a centralized polity and a growth of support for a decentralized one from waves 1 to 2 (although centralized still remains the largest category). However, similarly to other policies, waves 2 to 3 see a stabilization and even a slight reversal, as most of those switching from the pooled and reinsurance types go to the centralized type. The analysis of change shows similar patterns to other policies, as satisfaction with the EU increases the probability of remaining in the centralized category, and satisfaction with the national government decreases it. Differently from other policy areas, change in economic vulnerability has a positive effect on remaining in the centralized group.

6.1 Descriptives: General Preferences for Polity Types

Figure 22 shows the size of the group supporting each polity type when it comes to the defence domain. Similar to the other policy domains, the respondents preferring either a centralized polity (33.18 per cent) or a pooled polity (18.64 per cent) constitute a majority of respondents. This indicates that respondents have a strong preference for an EU army, whether in a centralized or pooled form, suggesting that there is a relatively strong coalitional basis for such an institutional reform at the EU level.

---

[17] See Table 10 for a comparative summary of findings across countries.

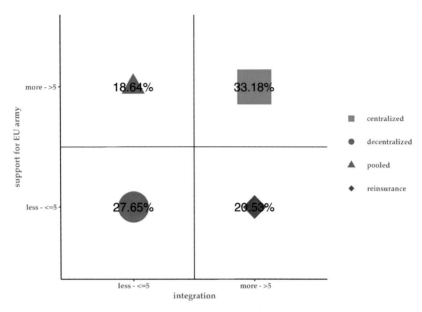

Figure 22 Polity versus policy attitudes on military policy

Nevertheless, the results also show high levels of preference for the decentralized and the reinsurance groups: 27.65 per cent of respondents express preferences for the former and 20.53 per cent of them for a reinsurance polity. The reinsurance group, pro-Europeans but skeptical of pooling resources, is the largest when compared to the size of this group in the other policy domains and, together, with the decentralized group, while still a minority, amounts to the biggest opposition towards centralization.

6.2 Territorial: Preferences for Polity Types by Country

Theoretical guidance on country preferences on military spending highlights three structuring dimensions: the context and the presence of a threat, the geographical proximity of the threat and the trade-off between guns and butter – that is between social and defence spending (Bartels 1994; Williams 2019; Barnum et al. 2024). In general, military spending preferences can be seen as a function of perceived external threat, which varies in time and space. Defence spending during the Cold War was much higher and much more supported than during the golden age of globalization (1989–2014), during which the 'peace dividend' allowed countries to dramatically reduce defence spending (apart from the United States, engaged in two wars). However, the rise of China as a strategic challenger and the resurgence of a revisionist Russia

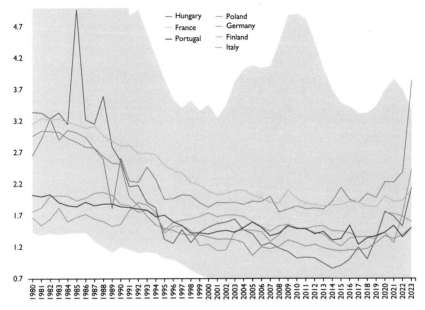

Figure 23 Defence spending in Western countries, in % of GDP

Data source: SIPRI Military Expenditure Database. The shaded area represents the range of spending in Western countries (minimum and maximum) for context. Western countries include: Austria, Belgium, Canada, Denmark, France, Germany, Greece, Ireland, Italy, the Netherlands, Norway, Portugal, Spain, Sweden, Switzerland, the United Kingdom, and the United States.

with the invasion of Ukraine in 2014 have ended this 'peace dividend' and have even spurred some divergences within NATO. Countries which are geographically close to a potential threat, such as the Baltic states and Poland, should witness a higher support for military spending. Finally, the literature also points to the theoretical trade-off between guns and butter: public preferences and actual spending on defence should decrease when the welfare state has a prominent place in the political economy of a country, especially in times of austerity (Hübscher, Sattler, and Truchlewski 2023). The evidence on this point is quite mixed however, as voters often internalize the Keynesian logic of defence spending (Williams 2019): every dollar or euro spent on defence generates jobs and growth which benefit the broader political economy.

Figure 23 suggests that some of these patterns hold. First, as the Cold War started to vanish in the rear-view mirror of history, military spending did decrease significantly and converged among countries to lower levels of GDP, especially after 2000 (the grey area represents the mean and ± standard

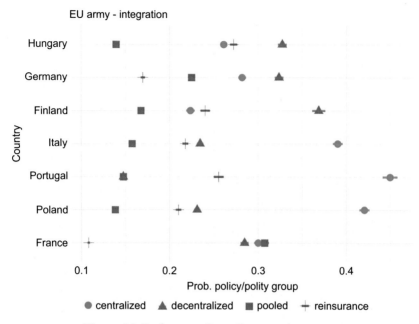

Figure 24 Preferences for polity types by country

deviation of Western countries). Second, military spending decreased faster and to lower levels in some countries than in others: take for instance landlocked Hungary, whose defence spending dropped below 1 per cent of GDP in 2014, or Germany, whose defence spending never increased beyond 1.4 per cent of GDP since 1997 (even after Russia attacked Ukraine in 2014). Their military spending is even lower than that of Portugal and Italy, who should not be threatened by a resurgent Russia. By contrast, other countries, like Russia-weary Poland, tried to maintain defence spending at around 2 per cent of GDP despite the tribulations of the post-communist transition. France followed the same goal due to the necessity to maintain its nuclear deterrent capacities and its role in forging security in Africa and the Middle-East. Finally, Finland does not fit the geography argument: its military spending does not reflect the perception of a Russian threat, which should be exacerbated by Finland's lack of NATO security until 2022. This is perhaps explained by the guns versus butter trade-off: countries with high social spending (Finland is in the top five, together with Italy and France[18]) should tend to have lower defence spending.

Figure 24 shows country-level preferences for polity types surrounding military policy. First, as suggested in the previous section, compared to other policy fields, respondents are much more lukewarm towards the centralized polity

---

[18] See https://data.oecd.org/socialexp/social-spending.htm.

but still form the largest group. In terms of territorial divides within the EU, three countries have the largest group of respondents preferring a decentralized polity: Hungary, Germany, and Finland. In both Hungary and Finland the reinsurance type of polity comes second, while in Germany the centralized polity comes second, suggesting a polarized electorate. By contrast, respondents in a second group of countries – the same as for foreign policy, that is, Italy, Portugal, and Poland – express clear preferences for a centralized polity for defence. This is somewhat counter-intuitive: neither Portugal nor Italy are directly threatened by a resurgent Russia. Poland is indeed, but is always perceived as putting its bets on NATO and aligning with the only credible military power, the United States. France is once more the idiosyncratic case: this is the only country where the pooled polity comes first. Respondents are almost equally divided into three groups, which points to difficult coalition-building of voters on the national level and a harder postfunctionalist constrain (30 per cent of respondents prefer a decentralized polity). However, a push for a European level army could be feasible if policymakers cobble a coalition out of respondents preferring a pooled or a centralized polity (slightly above 60 per cent of respondents).

All in all, countries where most respondents prefer a centralized or a pooled polity and form a majority that ease the postfunctional constraint are Italy (around 55 per cent), Portugal and France (around 60 per cent), and Poland (around 56 per cent). Countries where the coalition constrains on any form of pooling (decentralized and reinsurance preferences being highest) are Hungary and Finland (around 60 per cent).

6.3 Functional: The Effect of Individual Attitudes on Polity Types

We now move on to the multinomial results on the individual level. As for foreign policy, our previous results suggested that there is a significant amount of public support for an EU army which could be embedded into a centralized or a pooled polity. But which predictors on the individual-level shape support for each particular polity type?

We start with output legitimacy factors, displayed in Figure 25. Concerning satisfaction with military support for Ukraine, it appears that the more satisfied respondents are with aid, the more likely they are to prefer a centralized polity (when satisfaction increases from 0 to 10, support increases from a 20 per cent probability to a 50 per cent probability). In other words, support for a centralized polity increased 2.5 times. Conversely, support for a decentralized

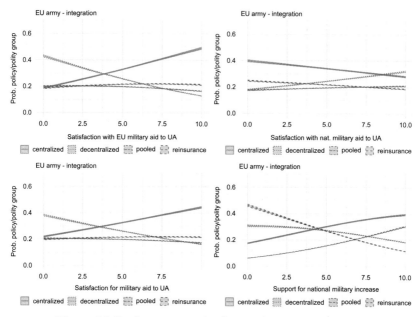

Figure 25 Performance evaluations and support – EU army

polity drops from 42.5 to 12.5 per cent, a decrease of 3.4 fold. Thus, satisfaction with EU aid to Ukraine has an asymmetric effects on polity preferences, the implication being that there is an important elasticity of satisfaction on polity type, as the potential support coalitions change dramatically in the two opposite ideal types (centralized vs. decentralized polity), but not in the pooled and reinsurance types of polity, which remain flat. We observe the same empirical patterns for general support for military aid to Ukraine, which reflects the results we obtained for the EU's foreign policy. Naturally, almost the opposite is observed with satisfaction for *national* aid to Ukraine: the more respondents are satisfied with it, the more they support a decentralized polity at the cost of a centralized one. This suggests that the way a polity responds to a crisis influences the preferences for the polity itself.

Next, we continue with the ideational and security factors shown in Figure 26. First, examining ideology we see that respondents from the centre and the left opt for a centralized and a reinsurance polity, while respondents from the right prefer a decentralized or a pooled polity. Next, the greater the threat, the greater the demand for a centralized polity and the lower the demand for a decentralized polity (note that whatever the threat level, the decentralized polity is never preferred). Furthermore, vulnerability also has an impact on the type of polity preferred: the effect on the two ideal types of polities goes in the expected direction (more vulnerability leads to higher preferences for a centralized polity

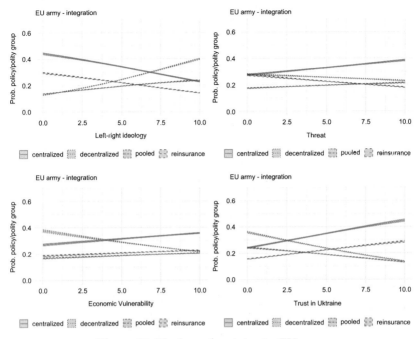

Figure 26 Ideology, threat, trust – EU army

Table 7 Changes in polity groups from waves 1 to 2 – EU army

Initial cat.	Centralized	Decentralized	Pooled	Reinsurance	N
1 Centralized	**64%**	7%	15%	15%	1,667
2 Decentralized	4%	**72%**	15%	9%	792
3 Pooled	18%	25%	**50%**	6%	692
4 Reinsurance	23%	27%	7%	**43%**	730

and lower preferences for a decentralized polity), while the effect on pooled and reinsurance polities is marginal. Trust in Ukraine has a similar impact (with the exception of the reinsurance polity, where the effect of trust in Ukraine is strong).

6.4 Dynamics over Time

We now consider the dynamics of change in preference for polity types over the course of the crisis. Table 7 shows that from waves 1 to 2, 64 per cent remained in the centralized category, with 7 per cent switching to decentralized, 15 per cent to pooled and 15 per cent to reinsurance. In contrast to the other policy fields, when it comes to the EU army, the decentralized group is the

Table 8 Changes in polity groups from waves 2 to 3 – EU army

Initial cat.	Centralized	Decentralized	Pooled	Reinsurance	N
1 Centralized	**70%**	4%	13%	13%	1,377
2 Decentralized	5%	**68%**	17%	11%	1,067
3 Pooled	23%	19%	**52%**	6%	745
4 Reinsurance	30%	16%	6%	**48%**	669

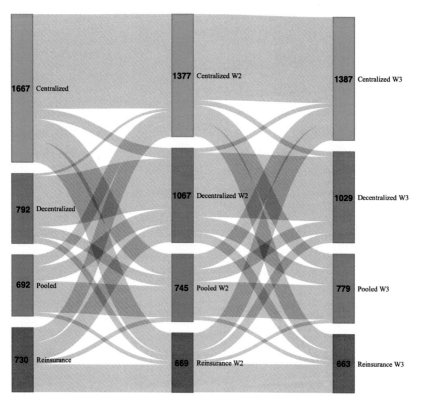

Figure 27 EU army change and stability across waves

most stable one. Thus, not only are respondents overall less likely to support a centralized polity for military policy, but they are also more likely to defect. However, similarly to other policy fields, we see a stabilization from waves 2 to 3 in Table 8, with the centralized group retaining its size and also gaining respondents from the pooled and reinsurance groups. These patterns can also be seen in Figure 27. Here we see the drastic decrease in centralized and increase in decentralized from waves 1 to 2, whereas waves 2 to 3 show a stabilization of centralized and a slight shrinking of decentralized. While in other policy

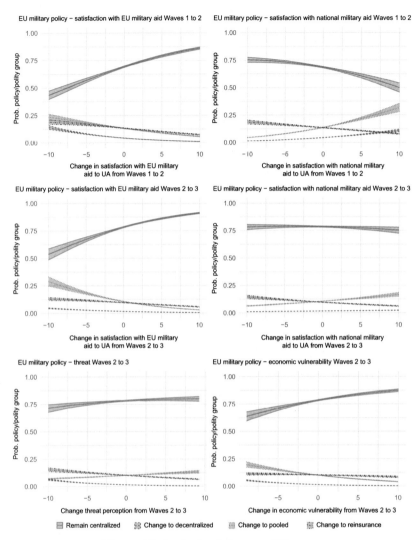

Figure 28 Analysis of change – EU army

fields reinsurance moved more towards centralized, in military policy in waves 1 to 2 more move from reinsurance to decentralized. This is reversed in waves 2 to 3, with both pooled and reinsurance switching more to centralized than decentralized.

In terms of the predictors of change, Figure 28 shows the predicted probability plot for the output legitimacy and security relate variables: satisfaction with EU and national military aid to Ukraine (both from waves 1 to 2 and 2 to 3) and threat and economic vulnerability (only waves 2 to 3). We see similar effects to those already shown in the foreign policy and energy policy domains. Growing satisfaction with EU military aid to Ukraine is associated with a drastic increase in the probability to stay in the centralized group, and a shrinking probability to switch to the others. Satisfaction with national military aid has the opposite effect, lowering the probability of staying in centralized or switching to reinsurance, and increasing the probability of switching to pooled, and to a lesser extent, to decentralized. Increasing one's satisfaction with national military aid to Ukraine therefore does not decrease support for the policy since respondents are more likely to prefer a pooled polity but less likely to prefer a reinsurance polity. Interestingly, and similarly to foreign policy and energy, satisfaction with national military aid is no longer predictive in waves 2 to 3. Unlike other policy fields, we note a substantive effect of change in economic hardship. Those who report being more greatly affected by rising energy prices in wave 3 compared to wave 2, are more likely to remain in the centralized category and less likely to switch to pooled.

6.5 Conclusion

Military policy stands out as the domain with the largest dissensus among the ones we study. Both the centralized and the pooled groups are considerably smaller than in other policy areas, although together they still form a narrow majority. As such, our results differ from a more optimistic literature that is confined to Western Europe (Burgoon, Van Der Duin, and Nicoli 2023). The small number of respondents favouring a pooled polity suggests that respondents cannot imagine pooling military competencies in a unified army without overall greater political integration. The fact that defence is a core state power may explain why it is much more polarizing for individuals. It may also explain why we see more territorial divisions. Our usual pro-centralized group of countries, Italy, Portugal, and Poland, contrast with Hungary, Germany, and Finland, which all have majorities for the decentralized type. France, on the other hand, is the most divided, with no clear majority. In terms of functional divides, we see similar patterns to other policy areas, as greater satisfaction with EU military aid increases the likelihood of supporting a centralized polity, while satisfaction with national aid decreases it. Differently from foreign policy, respondents who do not want to see any national military increase, that is, pacifists, are most in favour of a reinsurance polity, where they do not want to see military buildup at the EU level but support further political integration. Also differently from other policy fields, we see that both economic vulnerability and threat perception are positively related to supporting a centralized polity, albeit with smaller effects than other variables. When it comes to how opinions change over time, we note that military policy is also one of the most volatile. Only 64 per cent of those supporting a centralized polity in wave 1 remain supportive in wave 2. At the same time, a majority of those switching from supporting the pooled and reinsurance types go to the decentralized category. The result is a drastic shrinking of support for the centralized type and a growth of support for the decentralized one from waves 1 to 2. However, similarly to other policies, waves 2 to 3 see a stabilization and even a slight reversal as the centralized type gains in size. The analysis of change shows similar patterns to other policies, as satisfaction with the EU increases the probability of remaining supportive for the centralized type over time, while satisfaction with the national government decreases it. Differently from other policy areas, change in economic vulnerability has a positive effect on remaining in the centralized group.

7 Conclusions

7.1 Contributions to the Literature

In this Element, we set out to analyse the state of public opinion on the EU in the aftermath of the Russian invasion of Ukraine. We argued that focusing on public opinion is important given the politicization of the European polity and criticisms of its democratic deficit and weak voice channels. Conversely, a supportive public opinion can offer an enabling environment for policymaking at the EU level and could take the wind out of Euroskeptic parties' sails.

While this Element is definitely not the first to focus on public opinion in the EU in times of crises, it aims to bring several important contributions to this literature. These contributions have been inspired by the polity approach to the European Union (Bartolini 2005; Caramani 2015; Ferrera, Kriesi, and Schelkle 2024). The key insight that we take from the polity approach is that the building of the EU polity does not necessarily need to imply a full transfer or new creation of 'core' institutions to the EU at the expense of the Member States. By contrast, the authoritative centre of the EU can be further 'built' by, for example, improving the coordination between member states and further developing the compound polity where member states play first fiddles (Ferrera, Kriesi, and Schelkle 2024). Scholars have proposed concepts such as 'extensive unification' (Ferrera, Kyriazi, and Miró 2024; Truchlewski et al. 2025) or 'coordinative Europeanization' (Ladi and Wolff 2021) to refer to forms of polity building that do not necessarily imply a full centralization of powers at the EU level. We leverage this insight related to the variety of pathways that EU polity formation can take to further conceptualize demand-side support for the EU in two ways.

First, starting from the idea of the diversity of pathways that the EU polity formation can take, we also went beyond conceiving public support for the EU as uni-dimensional – that is, more or less pro-integration. For this, we proposed a new typology of public support for the EU that would allow us to capture a more diverse array of attitudes while maintaining parsimony. This typology conceives of EU support as playing out in two dimensions stemming from a distinction between 'policy' (specific) and 'polity' (diffuse) support (Easton 1975). By policy support, we refer to support for pooling resources and/or decisions at the EU level in specific policy domains. By polity support, we refer to a more general positive attitude toward the EU based on a deeper loyalty towards the polity. While the concepts of specific and diffuse EU support are not novel and have been related to one another in the literature, we argue that there is merit in studying their intersections rather than solely their (positive) correlation. Cross-tabulating these two dimensions opens a rich, four-fold analytical space in which public support for the EU can be categorized into four types: support for a centralized polity, a decentralized one, a pooled polity, or a reinsurance polity. While the existing literature assumes that the two attitudes go hand in hand, we have shown that what might be thought of as inconsistent views (wanting more EU integration but not wanting to centralize a specific policy or vice-versa) (Zaller 1992) are widespread. Indeed, we argue that these views are not inconsistent but point to alternative potential development pathways for the EU. A pooled polity would combine less direct political integration with more cooperation or coordination of specific policies. A reinsurance polity would combine more political integration with a decentralized approach to specific policies. We show that both groups are sizable and vary across policy fields. Our analysis, therefore, sheds light on two groups of citizens that are usually ignored in studies of EU support: those that support what we call a pooled polity and those that support a reinsurance type of polity.

The second theoretical assumption inspired by the polity approach that we started with and that guided our results was the fact that neither are crises monolithic threats nor do EU polity formation pathways need to be the same across policy domains. Our descriptive findings point to the utility of looking not only at attitudes towards the polity but also within each policy domain. Support for types of EU polity can vary across these domains as a function of the asymmetries that they exacerbate between countries and social groups, of the performance of European and Member state actors, or of previous attitudes. These factors drive out territorial divisions – between citizens in different Member States – and functional divisions – between groups of citizens across Member States.

The third contribution of the Element is to compare how respondents weight internal and external drivers of polity formation. The internal drivers refer to output legitimacy and ideology, while external drivers refer to security-related factors such as threats stemming from the invasion. As the classical

Table 9 Comparative results from descriptive preferences for polity types (percentage by polity type and policy domain)

Polity\Policy	Refugees	Energy	Foreign	Army
Centralized	39.8	39.5	38.9	33.2
Pooled	24.4	21.4	19.1	18.6
Reinsurance	13.9	15.1	15.6	20.5
Decentralized	21.8	23.9	26.4	27.6

field of European integration focused mainly on internal drivers, studying external drivers has gained prominence only more recently and particularly following the Russian invasion. As such, our contribution is a response to such recent debates about how wars shape polities and the European one in particular. Leveraging a classical argument in political science (Riker 1964; Tilly 1975), Kelemen and McNamara (2022) have argued that European polity formation is incomplete and that external threats like war would spur further centralization and capacity building. By contrast, Genschel (2022), Genschel, Leek, and Weyns (2023), Moise, Truchlewski, and Oana (2024) argue that this is not necessarily the case due to the compound nature of the European polity (Ferrera, Kriesi, and Schelkle 2024). Despite the deep intellectual aggiornamento that the Russian invasion in Ukraine has forced upon European elites (together with the American threat to withdraw from NATO), our results suggest that the external drivers of polity formation are still weaker than classical internal drivers. In what follows we further summarize these findings across policy domains.

7.2 Summary of Our Results

Our results underscore the complexity of the paths that lie ahead for the EU. When it comes to public opinion there are varying degrees of consensus for different types of polity formation. While across policy domains we see that the group preferring a centralized polity is the largest one, we show that respondents in each country are not necessarily split between preferring a centralized polity or a decentralized one, with a pooled polity or a reinsurance one being viable alternatives in all policy domains (see Table 11).

When comparing policy domains descriptively, we see that the refugee policy domain has the highest share of respondents supporting a centralized polity type (see Table 11). Importantly, for refugee policy, the pooled type is also the second-largest category. Taken together these groups imply that the refugee policy domain is the one where we can find the widest consensus in regards to

Table 10 Comparative results from territorial preferences for polity Types

Polity\Policy	Refugees	Energy	Foreign	Army
Centralized	DE*, FI*, IT, PT, PL	HU*, DE*, IT, PT, PL	HU*, DE*, IT, PT, PL	IT, PT, PL
Pooled Reinsurance	FR			FR
Decentralized	HU	FI, FR*	FR*, FI*	HU, DE, FI

NB: Countries with a star (*) have the most polarized respondents on the issue, for example, with one big group in favour of the decentralized polity and another big group in favour of the centralized polity in a given policy domain.

pooling resources and/or decisions at the EU level. This domain is followed by energy policy, foreign policy, and, finally, military policy, which has the lowest share of respondents preferring a centralized polity and the highest share preferring a decentralized one relative to other policies (yet note that it still has centralized as the largest group). What makes for a more permissive consensus in refugee and energy policy? One aspect might be that they do not involve giving up core state powers, as would be the case in the foreign policy and military fields. In both arenas EU security is enhanced by the fact that most EU member states belong to NATO, which provides external security, thus lessening the functional pressure on the EU.

In terms of territorial divides, we note important country differences among our respondents across policy fields. Thus, Table 10 shows the country divisions in terms of preferences for refugee policy are relatively muted, with only Hungary having a majority of respondents in favour of the decentralized polity and France having a majority for pooled, while the rest of the countries all have a plurality of respondents in favour of a centralized polity. Across the other three policy fields, we see a consistent 'pro-centralized polity coalition' formed by Poland, Portugal, and Italy. In energy and foreign policy, they are joined by Hungary and Germany. Military policy remains the most polarizing across countries. Finnish respondents, perhaps surprisingly, have a plurality for the decentralized polity. This might be surprising given Finland's geographical proximity to Russia and, hence, its higher threat level. However, as our individual results show, threat plays a minor role in driving support for polity types and its change over time.

When it comes to our static analyses, several patterns stand out (see Table 11). First, we note several similarities across policy fields. Support for polity types is driven not by external, security-related conditions, such as threat and economic vulnerability, but by internal, ideational and output

Table 11 Comparative results from functional preferences for polity types

Polity\Policy	Refugees	Energy	Foreign	Army
Centralized	Output	Output	Output	Output
	Ideational	Ideational	Ideational	Ideational
	Security	Security	Security	Security
Pooled	Output	Output	Output	Output
	Ideational	Ideational	Ideational	Ideational
	Security	Security	Security	Security
Reinsurance	Output	Output	Output	Output
	Ideational	Ideational	Ideational	Ideational
	Security	Security	Security	Security
Decentralized	Output	Output	Output	Output
	Ideational	Ideational	Ideational	Ideational
	Security	Security	Security	Security

NB: We put in the cells the factors that substantively impact the probability of choosing a polity category (in black). If they do not matter, they are in grey. We group out independent variables into three categories: Output (satisfaction with national and EU levels of government), Ideational (political ideology) and Security (threat and economic vulnerability).

legitimacy-related factors, including satisfaction with EU and national policy, ideology, and trust in Ukraine.[19] Importantly, quite stable across policy domains, satisfaction with the EU and national policy have strong effects on preferences for polity types and play opposite roles, the first being positively related to more polity centralization while the latter being negatively related. We note the same dynamic in our analysis of change between our three waves.[20] Taken together, these results suggest that within countries, preferences for these four polity types are more strongly rooted in output legitimacy and deep attitudinal variables rather than in factors directly related to the security or economic threats raised by the war when taking all attitudes into account. One exception

---

[19] Appendix Section 6 shows that the effects for threat and economic vulnerability remain largely the same even when excluding satisfaction with EU policy.

[20] We cannot conclusively prove with our data which way the causal arrow goes. It may be that those who are in favour of a centralized polity are more predisposed to be satisfied by EU policy. However, we note that our temporal analysis supports our interpretation. Given that polity attitudes shift less than satisfaction with policy, and that satisfaction with policy is more directly connected to the war and its evolution across time, we consider it plausible that changes in satisfaction drive changes in polity preferences. In the Appendix Figure 5.1 we show that even controlling for initial attitudes, changes in satisfaction are still strongly associated with polity attitudes. Irrespective of which way causality goes, our conclusion regarding the importance of satisfaction and ideational factors compared to security ones, which have almost no relationship with polity types net of the other factors, stands.

is military policy, where threat and economic vulnerability have significant effects even net of output legitimacy and ideational factors. In the military field, higher perceived threat and higher economic vulnerability increase the propensity towards the centralized polity type and decrease that towards the decentralized type.

Second, we also note important differences between policy domains. Most notably, refugee policy stands out as having the largest permissive consensus across ideological groups, as well as satisfaction with both the EU and national policy. Even at low levels of satisfaction with the EU and high levels of satisfaction with national policy, the centralized and pooled groups are the largest. At very high levels of satisfaction with the national government, the pooled group is similar in size to the centralized group. Military policy stands out as having the largest constraining dissensus and some of the largest heterogeneity by ideology and satisfaction, with right-wing respondents being more in favour of a decentralized polity and the left wing being split between centralized and reinsurance. Interestingly, pacifist respondents (who are completely against increasing national military capacity) are the only group that forms a majority for the reinsurance category. This is intuitive given that this group opposes not only national military increases but also increased military capacity and centralization at the EU level, while still supporting the EU polity in general. Since these individuals are more likely to be left-wing, this can explain the split we see in left-wing individuals in this policy field. The defence polity domain is, hence, the least likely case for centralization when looking at the demand side. Given that defence is a core state power and that (most) EU countries have external security guarantees through NATO, this is unsurprising.

Given the asymmetries in energy dependence and fiscal capacity, we note that energy policy also initially appeared to be a least likely case for high preferences for centralizing or pooling. However, as our analyses showed, security considerations played a minor role in attitude formation or change. This may explain why, despite the asymmetries, energy policy shows less conflict than what might be expected from an asymmetric policy, such as the case of the 2015 refugee crisis. The consensus on refugee sharing despite the asymmetric burden of Ukrainian refugees in 2022 shows that in certain instances, such asymmetries are not important when more powerful factors are at play such as output legitimacy, ideology, and views on the war.

Finally, when we look at our results over time we note that polity attitudes are not as stable as one might initially expect. Even in the short timeframe that we use here, from March to December 2022, we see intense volatility in polity preferences. The first months of the war saw many shifts in the political position of governments and the EU as policy adapted to the initial shock and to later developments in the war. Public opinion followed suit. Our results point to a decrease in support for a centralized polity from our waves 1 to 2, likely indicating an eroding rally-around-the-flag effect in line with previous results (Truchlewski, Oana, and Moise 2023). However, from waves 2 to 3, the size of support for each polity type begins to stabilize. One exception to this trend is again refugee policy, which saw a small reversal of the fading rally trend as the pro-centralized polity group grew larger in wave 3 while the pro-decentralized polity group shrank, 'losing' respondents to the pooled group.

Our temporal analysis of the centralized group confirmed our static findings from wave 2.[21] Growing satisfaction with the EU increased the probability of remaining in the centralized category, while growing satisfaction with national policy decreased it. In the case of refugee and energy policy, respondents who were very satisfied with the national government were more likely to switch from centralized to pooled, while for military policy this resulted in a gain for the decentralized group. Results for the change between waves 2 and 3 were broadly similar. For both foreign and military policy the second wave saw a fading of the effect of satisfaction with national military policy, with a small effect for energy policy. Similarly to our static analysis, the role of threat perceptions and economic vulnerability is limited. We note that growing economic vulnerability increases the probability of staying in the centralized group for military policy while increasing threat perception has a small positive effect on switching from centralized to reinsurance. Overall, however, it is again output legitimacy-related and ideational factors that are strongly related to changes in preference for polity types rather than external, security-related factors.

7.3 The Future of the EU after the Russian Invasion of Ukraine

What are the implications of our findings? First, our polity approach helps us to see that European politics are not frozen in a binary integration/anti-integration or pro/anti-EU cleavage, but rather that oftentimes respondents prefer different forms of polity formation that maximize the scale of the response to common problems without sacrificing sovereignty (e.g., pooled or reinsurance polity). A corollary of this proposition is that there is not necessarily a trade-off between European and national polity formation: strengthening one does not need to come at the expense of the other. Instead, we see a strong demand for the

---

[21] Section 4 of the Appendix shows results for the analysis of the other three groups, showing that effects are symmetric to those of the centralized group.

co-evolution of these two levels of the polity, where the European polity does not supersede the national one but enhances it.

Second and consequently, our results also underscore that there is a strong potential for coalitions among respondents. While the demand for a centralized polity is strongest, particularly, in those policy domains that do not involve core state powers (energy and refugee policy), in the foreign policy and defence domains Euroskeptical respondents do not necessarily all prefer the decentralized polity but demand, for instance, a pooled type of polity. This creates ample space for policymakers to 'craft' coalitions among their constituencies to gather support for policies that can shape the EU. For instance, policymakers and political elites seeing a need for further resource pooling in a policy domain can craft a coalition of respondents between the centralized and the pooled polity groups. Across all policy domains, these two groups together form a majority of respondents (as compared to the decentralized and reinsurance groups).

Third, such coalitions can lead to novel forms of centre building that do not necessarily entail a transfer of sovereignty but can rather involve novel forms of resource-pooling and risk-sharing. The key EU response to the COVID pandemic was the 'Next Generation EU' instrument which is a case in point of a compromise between those states that need solidarity and those that are reluctant to pay for it. The result is a temporary coordinated structure (for now) that pools common economic power to disburse fiscal stimulus to the national level (instead of centralizing it in Brussels). Likewise, military help to Ukraine is channelled through the European Peace Facility which reimburses Member States for the military hardware they transfer to Ukraine. Such flexibility in coalitions and forms of centre-building in the European polity enables a variety of polity pathways for the EU, pathways that can also vary across policy domains.

Fourth, the cost of this is that the EU is not necessarily bound to evolve as a coherent polity that can be designed ex-ante, but rather that the EU evolves piecemeal into a compound polity without a teleology or finalité along varying polity formation pathways by policy domains. This is the price to pay to assuage voters who may be skeptical of the EU and to avoid a strong backlash against integrationist leaps forward. The failed European Constitution of 2005 and the difficult ratification of the Lisbon Treaty have put such 'big bang' strategies to rest. However, the benefit of such a development is that the European Union can still form and reform as a polity even though crises may polarize its territorial and functional constituencies.

Finally, our results show that external threats do not automatically push public opinion to demand a more centralized polity in all policy fields. Despite the predictions of the 'bellicist' school of polity formation (Tilly 1975; Riker 1964;

Kelemen and McNamara 2021), leveraging a classical argument in political science, we rather see that internal drivers of polity formation are equally contributing to centralized polity preferences in all policies (while threat for instance only matters for foreign policy and defence). The external threat of Russian imperialism and war-mongering thus mostly operates through other channels than the security logic, as we show in this Element.

The fact that public opinion favours different forms of polity formation that are not the centralized ideal type also has implications in terms of which public goods the EU produces. The pooled and reinsurance types of polities suggest that public goods like energy or military security would still be produced at the national level, not the European one which would rather act as either a backstop or a coordination device. In other words, member states are responsible for their own public goods. If we see international organizations as clubs creating public goods, which therefore raise the costs of staying out (Anghel and Jones 2024), the implication is that the impact of Russia's war on Ukraine may perhaps undermine the procurement of centralized, truly common European goods.

References

Abbott, Kenneth W., Philipp Genschel, Duncan Snidal, and Bernhard Zangl. 2020. 'Competence–Control Theory: The Challenge of Governing through Intermediaries'. In *The Governor's Dilemma: Indirect Governance beyond Principals and Agents*, 3–36. Oxford: Oxford University Press.

Alt, James E., Jeffry Frieden, Michael J. Gilligan, Dani Rodrik, and Ronald Rogowski. 1996. 'The Political Economy of International Trade Enduring Puzzles and an Agenda for Inquiry'. *Comparative Political Studies* 29 (6): 689–717.

Altiparmakis, Argyrios, Sylvain Brouard, Martial Foucault, Hanspeter Kriesi, and Richard Nadeau. 2021. 'Pandemic Politics: Policy Evaluations of Government Responses to COVID-19'. *West European Politics* 44 (5–6): 1159–1179.

Anderson, Christopher J., and Jason D. Hecht. 2018. 'The Preference for Europe: Public Opinion about European Integration since 1952'. *European Union Politics* 19 (4): 617–638.

Anghel, Veronica, and Erik Jones. 2024. 'The Enlargement of International Organisations'. *West European Politics* 48 (1): 1–28.

Barnum, Miriam, Christopher J. Fariss, Jonathan N. Markowitz, and Gaea Morales. 2024. 'Measuring Arms: Introducing the Global Military Spending Dataset'. *Journal of Conflict Resolution*. https://doi.org/10.1177/0022 0027241232964

Bartels, Larry M. 1994. 'The American Public's Defense Spending Preferences in the Post-Cold War Era'. *Public Opinion Quarterly* 58 (4): 479–508.

Bartolini, Stefano. 2005. *Restructuring Europe: Centre Formation, System Building, and Political Structuring between the Nation State and the European Union*. Oxford: Oxford University Press.

Beetsma, Roel, Brian Burgoon, and Francesco Nicoli. 2023. 'Is European Attachment Sufficiently Strong to Support an EU Fiscal Capacity: Evidence from a Conjoint Experiment'. *European Journal of Political Economy* 78:102357. https://doi.org/10.1016/j.ejpoleco.2023.102357.

Blok, Lisanne de, Max Heermann, Julian Schuessler, Dirk Leuffen, and Catherine E. de Vries. 2024. 'All on Board? The Role of Institutional Design for Public Support for Differentiated Integration'. *European Union Politics*. 25(3), 593–604.

Bol, Damien, Marco Giani, André Blais, and Peter John Loewen. 2021. 'The Effect of COVID-19 Lock downs on Political Support: Some Good News for Democracy?' *European Journal of Political Research* 60 (2): 497–505.

Boomgaarden, Hajo G., Andreas R. T. Schuck, Matthijs Elenbaas, and Claes H. de Vreese. 2011. 'Mapping EU Attitudes: Conceptual and Empirical Dimensions of Euroscepticism and EU Support'. *European Union Politics* 12 (2): 241–266.

Bremer, Björn, Theresa Kuhn, Maurits Meijers, and Francesco Nicoli. 2023. 'In This Together? Support for European Fiscal Integration in the COVID-19 Crisis'. *Journal of European Public Policy* 31(9), 2582–2610.

Burgoon, Brian, Theresa Kuhn, Francesco Nicoli, and Frank Vandenbroucke. 2022. 'Unemployment Risk Sharing in the EU: How Policy Design Influences Citizen Support for European Unemployment Policy'. *European Union Politics* 23 (2): 282–308.

Burgoon, Brian, David Van Der Duin, and Francesco Nicoli. 2023. 'What Would Europeans Want a European Defence Union to Look Like?' Bruegel Working Paper (09).

Busemeyer, Marius R., Aurélien Abrassart, and Roula Nezi. 2021. 'Beyond Positive and Negative: New Perspectives on Feedback Effects in Public Opinion on the Welfare State'. *British Journal of Political Science* 51 (1): 137–162.

Buti, Marco, and Sergio Fabbrini. 2022. 'Next Generation EU and the Future of Economic Governance: Towards a Paradigm Change or Just a Big One-Off?' *Journal of European Public Policy* 31(9), 2582–2610.

Caramani, Daniele. 2015. *The Europeanization of Politics*. New York: Cambridge University Press.

Cederman, Lars-Erik, Paola Galano Toro, Luc Girardin, and Guy Schvitz. 2023. 'War Did Make States: Revisiting the Bellicist Paradigm in Early Modern Europe'. *International Organization* 77 (2): 324–362.

De Vries, Catherine E. 2018. De Vries, Catherine E. 2018. *Euroscepticism and the Future of European Integration*. Oxford: Oxford University Press.

Easton, David. 1975. 'A Re-Assessment of the Concept of Political Support'. *British Journal of Political Science* 5 (4): 435–457.

Eilstrup-Sangiovanni, Mette. 2022. 'The Anachronism of Bellicist State-Building'. *Journal of European Public Policy* 29 (12): 1901–1915.

Fabbrini, Sergio. 2022. 'Going beyond the Pandemic: "Next Generation Eu" and the Politics of Sub-Regional Coalitions'. *Comparative European Politics* 21: 64–81.

Ferrera, Maurizio. 2005. *The Boundaries of Welfare: European Integration and the New Spatial Politics of Social Protection*. Oxford: Oxford University Press.

Ferrara, Federico Maria, and Hanspeter Kriesi. 2021. 'Crisis Pressures and European Integration'. *Journal of European Public Policy* 29 (9): 1351–1373.

Ferrara, Federico Maria, Waltraud Schelkle, and Zbigniew Truchlewski. 2023. 'What Difference Does the Framing of a Crisis Make to EU Solidarity?' *European Union Politics* 24(4), 666–683.

Ferrera, Maurizio, Anna Kyriazi, and Joan Miró. 2024. 'Integration through Expansive Unification: The Birth of the European Health Union'. *Publius: The Journal of Federalism*. 54 (4, Fall): 711–736.

Ferrera, Maurizio, Hanspeter Kriesi, and Waltraud Schelkle. 2024. 'Maintaining the EU's Compound Polity during the Long Crisis Decade'. *Journal of European Public Policy* 31 (3): 706–728.

Ferrera, Maurizio, Joan Miró, and Stefano Ronchi. 2021. 'Walking the Road Together? EU Polity Maintenance during the COVID-19 Crisis'. *West European Politics* 44 (5–6): 1329–1352.

Ferrera, Maurizio, and Waltraud Schelkle. 2024. 'The Social Security Logic and the Formation of the European Polity'. *Paper in progress*.

Freudlsperger, Christian, and Frank Schimmelfennig. 2022. 'Transboundary Crises and Political Development: Why War Is Not Necessary for European State-Building'. *Journal of European Public Policy* 29 (12): 1871–1884.

Genschel, Philipp. 2022. 'Bellicist Integration? The War in Ukraine, the European Union and Core State Powers'. *Journal of European Public Policy* 29 (12): 1885–1900.

Genschel, Philipp and Markus Jachtenfuchs. 2013. Genschel, Philipp, and Markus Jachtenfuchs. 2013. 'Introduction: Beyond Market Regulation. Analysing the European Integration of Core State Powers'. In *Beyond the Regulatory Polity?: The European Integration of Core State Powers*, 1–23. Oxford: Oxford University Press.

2014. *Beyond the Regulatory Polity?: The European Integration of Core State Powers*. Oxford: Oxford University Press.

Genschel, Philipp, and Frank Schimmelfennig. 2022. 'War, Political Development, and European Integration: A Debate on Kelemen and McNamara's "State-Building and the European Union"'. *Journal of European Public Policy* 29 (12): 1867–1870.

Genschel, Philipp, Lauren Leek, and Jordy Weyns. 2023. 'War and Integration: The Russian Attack on Ukraine and the Institutional Development of the

EU'. *Journal of European Integration* 45 (3) (April): 343–360. Accessed 20 July 2023.

Gourevitch, Peter. 1978. 'The Second Image Reversed: The International Sources of Domestic Politics'. *International Organization* 32 (4): 881–912.

Haas, Ernst. 1958. *Uniting of Europe: Political, Social, and Economic Forces, 1950–1957*. Notre Dame: University of Notre Dame Press.

Hacker, Jacob S., and Paul Pierson. 2014. 'After the "Master Theory": Downs, Schattschneider, and the Rebirth of Policy-Focused Analysis'. *Perspectives on Politics* 12 (3): 643–662.

Hemerijck, Anton, Philipp Genschel, Dietlind Stolle et al. 2022. *EUI-YouGov SiE Survey on Solidarity in Europe: Trendfile and Yearly Datasets*. Accessed 26 April 2023.

Hintze, Otto. 1975. *The Historical Essays of Otto Hintze*. Edited by Felix Gilbert. New York: Oxford University Press.

Hirschman, Albert O. 1970. *Exit, Voice, and Loyalty Responses to Decline in Firms, Organizations, and States*. Cambdrige, MA: Harvard University Press.

Hix, Simon, and Bjørn Høyland. 2024. 'The Dance of European Integration: How Ideology and Policy Shape Support for the EU'. *Paper in progress*.

Holzinger, Katharina, and Frank Schimmelfennig. 2012. 'Differentiated Integration in the European Union: Many Concepts, Sparse Theory, Few Data'. *Journal of European Public Policy* 19 (2): 292–305.

Hooghe, Marc, and Britt Wilkenfeld. 2008. 'The Stability of Political Attitudes and Behaviors across Adolescence and Early Adulthood: A Comparison of Survey Data on Adolescents and Young Adults in Eight Countries'. *Journal of Youth and Adolescence* 37 (2): 155–167.

Hooghe, Liesbet, and Gary Marks. 2009. 'A Postfunctionalist Theory of European Integration: From Permissive Consensus to Constraining Dissensus'. *British Journal of Political Science* 39 (1) (January): 1–23. Accessed 3 May 2023.

2018. 'Cleavage Theory Meets Europe's Crises: Lipset, Rokkan, and the Transnational Cleavage'. *Journal of European Public Policy* 25 (1): 109–135.

2019. 'Grand Theories of European Integration in the Twenty-first Century'. *Journal of European Public Policy* 26 (8): 1113–1133.

Hübscher, Evelyne, Thomas Sattler, and Zbigniew Truchlewski. 2023. 'Three Worlds of Austerity: Voter Congruence over Fiscal Trade-offs in Germany, Spain and the UK'. *Socio-Economic Review* 21 (2): 959–983.

Jones, Erik. 2009. 'Output Legitimacy and the Global Financial Crisis: Perceptions Matter'. *JCMS: Journal of Common Market Studies* 47 (5): 108–1105.

Kelemen, R. Daniel. 2011. *Eurolegalism: The Transformation of Law and Regulation in the European Union*. Cambridge, MA: Harvard University Press.

Kelemen, R. Daniel, and Kathleen R. McNamara. 2021. 'State-building and the European Union: Markets, War, and Europe's Uneven Political Development'. *Comparative Political Studies* 55 (6): 18–34.

——— 2022. 'State-building and the European Union: Markets, War, and Europe's Uneven Political Development'. *Comparative Political Studies* 55 (6): 963–991.

Kriesi, Hanspeter, Sven Hutter, and Edgar Grande. 2016. *Politicising Europe: Integration and Mass Politics*. Cambridge: Cambridge University Press.

Kriesi, Hanspeter, Alexandru D. Moise, and Ioana-Elena Oana. 2024. 'The Determinants of Transnational Solidarity within the EU'. *West European Politics*. https://doi.org/10.1080/01402382.2024.2340336

Kriesi, Hanspeter, Argyrios Altiparmakis, Abel Bojar, and Ioana-Elena Oana. 2024. *Coming to Terms with the European Refugee Crisis*. Cambridge: Cambridge University Press.

Ladi, Stella, and Sarah Wolff. 2021. 'The EU Institutional Architecture in the Covid-19 Response: Coordinative Europeanization in Times of Permanent Emergency'. *Journal of Common Market Studies* 59 (S1): 32–43.

Leruth, Benjamin, Stefan Gänzle, and Jarle Trondal. 2019. 'Exploring Differentiated Disintegration in a Post-Brexit European Union'. *JCMS: Journal of Common Market Studies* 57 (5): 1013–1030.

Leuffen, Dirk, Julian Schuessler, and Jana Gómez Díaz. 2022. 'Public Support for Differentiated Integration: Individual Liberal Values and Concerns about Member State Discrimination.' *Journal of European Public Policy* 29 (2): 218–237.

Levitsky, Steven, and Daniel Ziblatt. 2023. *Tyranny of the Minority: Why American Democracy Reached the Breaking Point*. New York: Crown.

Lipset, Seymour Martin, and Stein Rokkan. 1967. *Party Systems and Voter Alignments: Cross-national Perspectives*. International yearbook of political behavior research. New York, NY: Free Press.

Madlovics, Bálint, and Bálint Magyar. 2023. 'Hungary's Dubious Loyalty: Orbán's Regime Strategy in the Russia-Ukraine War'. In *Russia's Imperial Endeavor and Its Geopolitical Consequences,* edited by Bálint Madlovics and Bálint Magyar, 255–286. Budapest: The Russia-Ukraine War, Volume

Two. Central European University Press. Accessed November 27, 2023. https://doi.org/10.7829/jj.3985460.15.

Mann, Michael. 2012. *The Sources of Social Power: Volume 2: The Rise of Classes and Nation-States, 1760–1914.* Cambridge: Cambridge University Press. https://doi.org/10.1017/CBO9781139381314.

Matthijs, Matthias, and Kathleen McNamara. 2015. 'The Euro Crisis Theory Effect: Northern Saints, Southern Sinners, and the Demise of the Eurobond'. *Journal of European Integration* 37 (2): 229–245.

Midford, Paul. 1993. 'International Trade and Domestic Politics: Improving on Rogowski's Model of Political Alignments'. *International Organization* 47 (4): 535–564.

Milward, Alan S., George Brennan, and Federico Romero. 1992. *The European Rescue of the Nation State.* Berkeley: University of California Press.

Moise, Alexandru D., James Dennison, and Hanspeter Kriesi. 2023. 'European Attitudes to Refugees after the Russian Invasion of Ukraine'. *West European Politics* 47(2, July), 356–381.

Moise, Alexandru D., Marcello Natili, Ioana-Elena Oana et al. 2023. 'Introduction: EU Polity Building after the Russian Invasion of Ukraine'. *Journal of European Public Policy* 30 (8): 1657–1661.

Moise, Alexandru D., Ioana-Elena Oana, Zbigniew Truchlewski, and Chendi Wang. 2024. 'Two Functionalist Logics of EU Polity Building under External Threat: Evidence from a Conjoint Experiment'. *European Union Politics* Forthcoming.

Moise, Alexandru D., Zbigniew Truchlewski, and Ioana-Elena Oana. 2024. 'Tilly versus Milward: Experimental Evidence of Public Preferences for European Defense Amidst the Russian Threa'. *Political Behavior.* https://doi.org/10.1007/s11109-024-09979-x.

Mueller, John E. 1970. 'Presidential Popularity from Truman to Johnson'. *American Political Science Review* 64 (1): 18–34.

1973. *War, Presidents, and Public Opinion.* New York: Wiley.

Natili, Marcello, and Francesco Visconti. 2023. A Different Logic of Polity Building? The Russian Invasion of Ukraine and EU Citizens' Demand for Social Security, *Journal of European Public Policy*, 30 (8): 1699–1713, https://doi.org/10.1080/13501763.2023.2217228.

Nicoli, Francesco, David van der Duin, Roel Beetsma et al. 2024. 'Closer during Crises? European Identity during the COVID-19 Pandemic and the Russian Invasion of Ukraine'. Journal of European Public Policy 31(10): 3066–3092. https://doi.org/10.1080/13501763.2024.2319346,

Nicoli, Francesco, David van der Duin, and Brian Burgoon. 2023. 'Which Energy Security Union? An Experiment on Public Preferences for Energy

Union Alternatives in 5 Western European Countries'. *Energy Policy* 183: 113734. https://doi.org/10.1016/j.enpol.2023.113734.

Oana, Ioana-Elena, Alexandru D. Moise, and Zbigniew Truchlewski. 2024. 'Demand-side Constrains on European Solidarity for Energy Sanctions: Experimental Evidence from Seven EU Countries'. *European Union Politics* Forthcoming.

Oana, Ioana-Elena, and Zbigniew Truchlewski. 2024. 'Bounded Solidarity? Experimental Evidence on Cross-national Bonding in the EU during the COVID Crisis'. *European Journal of Political Research* 63 (3): 815–838.

Pavone, Tommaso. 2022. *The Ghostwriters: Lawyers and the Politics behind the Judicial Construction of Europe.* Cambridge: Cambridge University Press.

Pierson, Paul. 1996. 'The Path to European Integration: A Historical Institutionalist Analysis'. *Comparative Political Studies* 29 (2): 123–163.

Porte, Caroline de la, and Mads Dagnis Jensen. 2022. 'The Next Generation EU: An Analysis of the Dimensions of Conflict behind the Deal'. *Social Policy & Administration* 55 (2): 388–402.

Riker, William H. 1964. *Federalism : Origin, Operation, Significance.* Boston: Little, Brown.

Rogowski, Ronald. 1989. *Commerce and Coalitions: How Trade Affects Domestic Political Alignments.* Princeton: Princeton University Press.

Rokkan, Stein, Peter Flora, Stein Kuhnle, and Derek Urwin. 1999. *State Formation, Nation-building, and Mass Politics in Europe: The Theory of Stein Rokkan.* Oxford: Oxford University Press.

Scharpf, Fritz W. 1999. *Governing in Europe: Effective and Democratic?* Oxford: Oxford University Press.

Schelkle, Waltraud. 2014. 'The Insurance Potential of a Non-optimal Currency Area'. In *Democratic Politics in a European Union under Stress,* edited by Olaf Cramme and Sara B. Hobolt, 137–154. Oxford: Oxford University Press.

2017. *The Political Economy of Monetary Solidarity: Understanding the Euro Experiment.* Oxford: Oxford University Press.

Schelkle, Waltraud. 2022. 'The Political Economy of Reinsurance'. In *The Cambridge Handbook on European Monetary, Economic and Financial Market Integration,* edited by Dariusz Adamski, Fabian Amtenbrink, and Jakob de Haan, 125–138. Cambridge: Cambridge University Press.

2023a. 'Monetary Integration, Crises, and Solidarity'. In *European Political Economy: Theoretical Approaches and Policy Issues,* edited by Manuela

Moschella, Lucia Quaglia, and Aneta Spendzharova, 115–136. Oxford: Oxford University Press.

2023b. 'Monetary Re-insurance of Fiscal States in Europe'. *Stato e Mercato* 127 : 29–52.

Schimmelfennig, Frank, Dirk Leuffen, and Catherine E. De Vries. 2023. 'Differentiated Integration in the European Union: Institutional Effects, Public Opinion, and Alternative Flexibility Arrangements'. *European Union Politics* 24 (1): 3–20.

Schmidt, Vivien A. 2013. 'Democracy and Legitimacy in the European Union Revisited: Input, Output and "Throughput"'. *Political Studies* 61 (1): 2–22.

Schraff, Dominik. 2021. 'Political Trust during the Covid-19 Pandemic: Rally around the Flag or Lockdown Effects?' *European Journal of Political Research* 60 (4): 1007–1017.

Schüssler, Julian, Max Heermann, Dirk Leuffen, Lisanne de Blok, and Catherine E. De Vries. 2023. 'Mapping Public Support for the Varieties of Differentiated Integration'. *European Union Politics* 24 (1): 164–183.

Steiner, Nils D., Ruxanda Berlinschi, Etienne Farvaque et al. 2023. 'Rallying around the EU Flag: Russia's Invasion of Ukraine and Attitudes toward European Integration'. *JCMS: Journal of Common Market Studies* 61 (2): 283–301. Accessed 29 February 2024.

Stepan, Alfred C. 1999. 'Federalism and Democracy: Beyond the U.S. Model'. *Journal of Democracy* 10 (4): 19–34.

Strayer, Joseph R. 1970. *On the Medieval Origins of the Modern State*. Princeton: Princeton University Press.

Tilly, Charles, ed. 1975. *The Formation of National States in Western Europe*. 1st ed. Princeton: Princeton University Press, July.

1985. 'War Making and State Making as Organized Crime'. In *Bringing the State Back In*, edited by Peter Evans, Dietrich Rueschemeyer, and Theda Skocpol, 169–186. Cambridge: Cambridge University Press.

1990. *Coercion, Capital, and European States, AD 990–1990*. Oxford: Basil Blackwell.

Truchlewski, Zbigniew, Ioana-Elena Oana, and Alexandru D. Moise. 2023. 'A Missing Link? The European Polity and the Rally-round-the-flag after the Russian Invasion of Ukraine'. *Journal of European Public Policy* 30 (8) : 1662–1678.

Truchlewski, Zbigniew, Ioana-Elena Oana, Alexandru D. Moise, and Hanspeter Kriesi. 2025. *Pandemic Polity: How COVID-19 Contributed to Building the European Polity in the EU*. Oxford: Oxford University Press.

Truchlewski, Zbigniew, Ioana-Elena Oana, and Marcello Natili. 2024. 'Undersanding Public Support for EU Polity Building in Hard Times: The Role of Territorial, Functional, and Crisis Politics'. *Paper in progress.*

Vollaard, Hans. 2014. 'Explaining European Disintegration'. *JCMS: Journal of Common Market Studies* 52 (5): 1142–1159.

Vries, Catherine E. De, and Erica E. Edwards. 2009. 'Taking Europe to Its Extremes: Extremist Parties and Public Euroscepticism'. *Party Politics* 15 (1): 5–28.

Wang, Chendi, and Alexandru D. Moise. 2023. 'A Unified Autonomous Europe? Public Opinion of the EU's Foreign and Security Policy'. *Journal of European Public Policy* 30 (8) (May): 1679–1698. Accessed 30 May 2023.

Wheeler, Nicholas C. 2011. 'The Noble Enterprise of State Building: Reconsidering the Rise and Fall of the Modern State in Prussia and Poland'. *Comparative Politics* 44 (1): 21–38.

Williams, Laron K. 2019. 'Guns Yield Butter? An Exploration of Defense Spending Preferences'. *Journal of Conflict Resolution* 63 (5): 1193–1221.

Zaller, John R. 1992. *The Nature and Origins of Mass Opinion.* New York: Cambridge University Press.

Acknowledgements

This work was supported by the European Research Council, g.n. 810356, project Policy Crisis and Crisis Politics. Sovereignty, Solidarity and Identity in the EU post 2008 – SOLID. We wish to thank our colleagues in the SOLID project for feedback and support while drafting this manuscript, especially Hanspeter Kriesi and Dániel Kovarek.

Cambridge Elements ☰

European Politics

Catherine De Vries
Bocconi University

Catherine De Vries is a Dean of International Affairs and Professor of Political Science at Bocconi University. Her research revolves around some of the key challenges facing the European continent today, such as Euroscepticism, political fragmentation, migration and corruption. She has published widely in leading political science journals, including the American Political Science Review and the Annual Review of Political Science. She has published several books, including Euroscepticism and the Future of European integration (Oxford University Press), received the European Union Studies Association Best Book in EU Studies Award, and was listed in the Financial Times top-5 books to read about Europe's future.

Gary Marks
University of North Carolina at Chapel Hill and European University Institute

Gary Marks is Burton Craige Professor at the University of North Carolina Chapel Hill, and Professor at the European University Institute, Florence. He has received the Humboldt Forschungspreis and the Daniel Elazar Distinguished Federalism Scholar Award. Marks has been awarded an Advanced European Research Council grant (2010–2015) and is currently senior researcher on a second Advanced European Research Council grant. He has published widely in leading political science journals, including the American Political Science Review and the American Journal of Political Science. Marks has published a dozen books, including A Theory of International Organization and Community, Scale and Regional Governance.

Advisory Board

About the Series

The Cambridge Elements Series in European Politics will provide a platform for cutting-edge comparative research on Europe at a time of rapid change for the disciplines of political science and international relations. The series is broadly defined, both in terms of subject and academic discipline. The thrust of the series will be thematic rather than ideographic. It will focus on studies that engage key elements of politics — e.g. how institutions work, how parties compete, how citizens participate in politics, how laws get made.

Cambridge Elements ≡

European Politics

Elements in the Series

Political Change and Electoral Coalitions in Western Democracies
Peter A. Hall, Georgina Evans and Sung In Kim

Cleavage Formation in the 21st Century: How Social Identities Shape Voting Behavior in Contexts of Electoral Realignment
Simon Bornschier, Lukas Haffert, Silja Häusermann, Marco Steenbergen and Delia Zollinger

Crisis Policymaking in the EU: The Covid-19 Crisis and the Refugee Crisis 2015-16 Compared
Hanspeter Kriesi

The European Ideological Space in Voters' Own Words
Noam Gidron and Thomas Tichelbaecker

Demand for EU Polity Building in the Shadow of the Russian Threat
Ioana-Elena Oana, Alexandru D. Moise and Zbigniew Truchlewski

A full series listing is available at: www.cambridge.org/EEP

Printed in the United States
by Baker & Taylor Publisher Services